5-Minute English

APA Publications (UK) Limited

New York   London   Singapore

5–MINUTE ENGLISH

Contacting the Editors
Every effort has been made to provide accurate information in this publication, but changes are inevitable. The publisher cannot be responsible for any resulting loss, inconvenience or injury. We would appreciate it if readers would call our attention to any errors or outdated information by contacting Berlitz Publishing, comments@ berlitzpublishing.com.

Berlitz Trademark Reg. U.S. Patent Office and other countries. Marca Registrada. Used under license from Berlitz Investment Corporation.

First Printing: June 2011
Printed in China
ISBN 978-981-268-859-0

Publishing Director: Sheryl Olinsky Borg
Senior Editor/Project Manager: Lorraine Sova, Monica Bentley
Cover Design: Leighanne Tillman
Interior Composition: Wee Design Group
Production Manager: Elizabeth Gaynor
Cover Illustration: ©2006 iStockphoto.com/Art–Y/Helle Bro Clemmensen

Contents

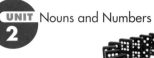 **UNIT 1** Saying Hello and Introductions

 UNIT 2 Nouns and Numbers

 **UNIT 3** Time and Date

 UNIT 4 Family

 UNIT 5 Meals

 UNIT 6 Weather and Temperature

Contents

How to Use This Book

By using *5-Minute English* every day, you can start speaking English in just minutes. The 5-Minute program introduces you to a new language and gets you speaking right away. Take a few minutes before or after work, before you go to sleep at night or any time that feels right to work on one lesson a day. If you want, you can even go ahead and do two lessons a day. Just have fun while you learn; you'll be speaking English in no time.

- The book is divided into 99 lessons. Each provides a bite-sized learning opportunity that you can complete in minutes.

- Each unit has 8 lessons presenting important vocabulary, phrases and other information needed in everyday English.

- A review at the end of each unit provides an opportunity to test your knowledge before you move on.

Hello!

- Real-life language and activities introduce the vocabulary, phrases and grammar covered in the lessons that follow. You'll see dialogues, postcards, e-mails and other everyday correspondence in English.

- You can listen to the dialogues, articles, e-mails and other presentations on the *5-Minute English* audio CD.

Smart Phrases

- In these lessons you'll find useful everyday phrases. You can listen to these phrases on the audio program.

- Extra Phrases enrich your knowledge and understanding of everyday English. These are not practiced in the activities, but they're there for those who want to learn.

5-Minute English audio
When you see this symbol , you'll know to listen to the specified track on the *5-Minute English* audio CD.

Words to Know

- Essential Words are important words related to the lesson topic. In some lessons these words are divided into sub-categories. You can listen to these words on our audio program.

- Extra Words are other helpful words to know.

SMART TIP

Boxes like these are here to extend your English knowledge. You'll find differences in English from country to country, extra language conventions and other helpful information on how to speak better English.

Smart Grammar

- Don't let the name scare you. Smart Grammar covers the basic parts of speech you'll need to know if you want to speak English easily and fluently.

- From verb usage to forming questions, the 5-Minute program provides quick and easy explanations and examples for how to use these structures.

CULTURE TIP

Boxes like these introduce useful cultural information about English-speaking countries.

Unit Review   Here you'll have a chance to practice what you've learned.

Challenge
Extend your knowledge even further with a challenge activity.

SMART PRONUNCIATION

Boxes like these demonstrate specific pronunciation tools.

Internet Activity

- Internet activities take you to **www.berlitzpublishing.com**, where you can test drive your new language skills. Just look for the computer symbol.

Unit 1 Saying Hello and Introductions

In this unit you will learn:
- greetings.
- to say your name and where you're from.
- personal pronouns and the verb *to be*.
- to talk about nationalities and countries.

Hello!

Dialogue

Lisa meets her new neighbor, Jake. Listen to their conversation.

Lisa Good morning! My name is Lisa. What's your name?

Jake My name's Jake. Nice to meet you.

Lisa I'm from England. Where are you from?

Jake I'm from the United States.

Lisa I'm sorry, I have to go. Goodbye.

Jake Me too. Bye!

SMART TIP

Notice the forms *'m* and *'s* in the dialogue. These are contracted forms of the verb *to be*, which are shortened and attached to personal pronouns: *I'm* (for *I am*), *My name's Lisa* (for *My name is Lisa*).

Activity A

Circle **T** for true and **F** for false.

1 This meeting takes place during the day. **T** / F
2 Jake is happy to meet Lisa. T / F
3 Lisa is from Canada. T / F
4 Jake is from the United States. T / F

Activity B

Complete the conversation. Use sentences and questions from the dialogue.

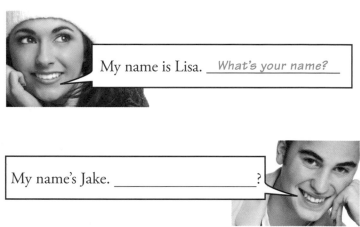

My name is Lisa. *What's your name?*

My name's Jake. _____?

I'm from England. _____.

I'm from _____.

CULTURE TIP

In the United Kingdom and the United States, people often shake hands on first meeting. They rarely kiss when they first meet. They show that they are happy to meet people through facial expressions more than by gestures. Americans often greet one another with a smile, even if they don't know each other!

SMART TIP

In English, people greet each other in different ways throughout the day: *Good morning* in the morning, *Good afternoon* in the afternoon, *Good evening* in the evening and *Good night* at night. *Good night* is used only when people leave. The others are used when people arrive.

Essential Phrases

Hello!/Hi!
Goodbye!/Bye!
Good morning.
Good afternoon.
Good evening.
Good night.
I am.../I'm...
It is.../It's...
What is/What's your name?
Where are you from?
Nice to meet you.
I'm sorry.
I have to go.
Me too.

SMART TIP

Good news: English is easier than some other languages! In fact, there are no formal or informal forms of address. *You* addresses one or more people in all situations.

Activity A

What do you say if you want to…

1   …greet someone?
    Hello! / Hi!

2   …ask someone's name?

3   …ask where someone comes from?

4   …leave someone?

5   …say that you have to leave?

Activity B

Write the correct greeting for each picture. Choose from *Good morning, Good afternoon* or *Good night*.

1 _____

2 _____

3 _____

SMART TIPS

- In English, the names of countries don't have *the* in front of them, except if they're part of a group of many territories or states like *the United States* or *the United Kingdom*.
- To help you remember country names in English, make flash cards with flags on one side and the country name on the back. Say the names out loud regularly.
- See page ~~306~~ for a list of countries and nationalities.

Essential Words

Australia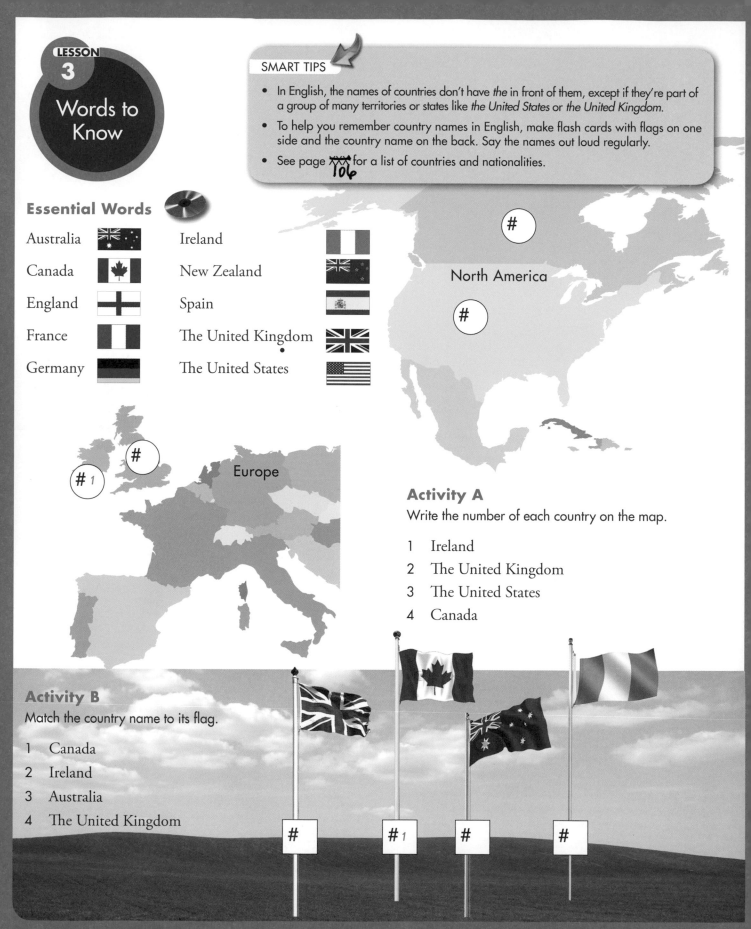

Canada

England

France

Germany

Ireland

New Zealand

Spain

The United Kingdom

The United States

North America

Europe

Activity A
Write the number of each country on the map.

1   Ireland
2   The United Kingdom
3   The United States
4   Canada

Activity B
Match the country name to its flag.

1   Canada
2   Ireland
3   Australia
4   The United Kingdom

Smart Grammar

SMART TIPS

- The singular personal pronoun *it* can talk about an object or an animal. With pets *he* or *she* is used instead of *it*.
- The plural personal pronoun *they* talks about a group of men and/or women (and/or objects or animals). *They* is neither masculine nor feminine.

Personal Pronouns

I
you (sing.)
he (m.)/she (f.)/it (objects and animals)
we
you (pl.)
they (m./f. pl.)

Abbreviations

British English	(Brit.)	American English	(Am.)
masculine	(m.)	feminine	(f.)
singular	(sing.)	plural	(pl.)

Activity A

Give the singular personal pronoun for each image.

1 _____ *I*

2 _____

3 _____

4 _____

Activity B

Give the plural personal pronoun for each image.

1 _____ *they*   2 _____

3 _____

Activity C

Which personal pronoun do you use to talk about…

1 …yourself?   *I* _____

2 …a woman?   _____

3 …a man?   _____

4 …a group of women?   _____

5 …a group of people?   _____

Where are you from?

Language and Nationality

English is the first language or one of the official languages in more than 70 countries. It is the first language in Australia, Jamaica, New Zealand, the United Kingdom and the United States, for example. It is an official language in Cameroon, Canada, Ghana, India, Ireland, Kenya, Hong Kong, Nigeria, Pakistan, the Philippines, South Africa, Uganda and lots more. People often speak English in Bahrain, Israel, Malaysia and the United Arab Emirates. Globally, one out of four people speaks at least a little English. It is also the main language for airports and air-traffic control, sports, international business and academic conferences, science, diplomacy, pop music and international competitions!

Country	Nationality	Language
United Kingdom	British	English
England	English	English
Ireland	Irish	English
United States	American	English
Canada	Canadian	English
Australia	Australian	English

English-Speaking Countries

Read and listen to the article on English-speaking countries. Don't worry if you don't understand right away! Try to understand the overall meaning of the text. Underline the words you do not understand in the text. Look for words that are similar in your language.

Activity A

Complete the table below with examples from the article.

country	The United States	The United Kingdom
language		
nationality		

Activity B

Read the article again. Circle the correct answer.

1   English is the official language in more than 70…
    a countries   **b populations**

2   In Jamaica, people speak…
    a English   **b Jamaican**

3   One in four people in the world has a little knowledge of…
    a American   **b English**

4   English is the language of…
    a diplomatics   **b diplomacy**

SMART TIP

In English, words that talk about nationality and names of languages start with a capital letter.

I'm English. She's Canadian. She speaks French.

LESSON 6

Words to Know

Essential Words

American	🇺🇸	Indian	
Brazilian	🇧🇷	Italian	
Chinese	🇨🇳	Korean	
Colombian		Mexican	🇲🇽
English		Spanish	
Filipino		Vietnamese	

Activity A

Give the nationality of each flag.

1 This is a _____*Canadian*_____ flag.
Canadian/Chinese

2 This is a _____ flag.
Korean /Mexican

3 This is an _____ flag.
Indian/English

4 This is a _____ flag.
Filipino/Vietnamese

Activity B

Give the nationality of each food. Use the vocabulary below.

English	**Spanish**	**American**
French	**Italian**	

1 _____*Spanish*_____

2 _____

3 _____

4 _____

5 _____

> **SMART TIPS**
>
> - In English, the adjective comes before the noun. English adjectives only have one form—they do not agree in gender (masculine/feminine) or in number (singular/plural).
>
>   For example: *the rich man, a red car, the big houses, English tea.*
>
> - The words for nationalities do not change for masculine/feminine. For example: *He is Australian. She is Australian.*

Smart Phrases

Essential Phrases

Are you American?

Are you English?

I'm Canadian.

Do you speak English?

I speak a little.

I'm not very good./I don't speak it well.

Activity A

What do you say if you want to…

1 …say that you're from France?
   I'm French.
   _____

2 …ask someone if he is English?
   _____

3 …say you don't speak English very well?
   _____

4 …say that you speak English very little?
   _____

Your Turn

Imagine that you are on a trip to the United Kingdom. You meet a new person. Write a dialogue with the words and phrases in this lesson. Ask the person about his or her nationality and what language he or she speaks. Write your questions in the "You" column and the responses in the column labeled "A British Person."

You	A British Person
Question 1:	Answer 1:
Question 2:	Answer 2:

CULTURE TIP

How are you doing? People often greet each other with this phrase in the United States. The usual answer is, *"I'm fine. And you?"* It's used to start a conversation. Give it a try!

CULTURE TIPS

- The United Kingdom includes Great Britain (England, Scotland and Wales) and Northern Ireland.
- The United States is a country of immigration. The country was created upon the arrival of many immigrants who came to a new world. Many Americans add another nationality adjective before "American" to indicate their national origin: *Mexican-American, Chinese-American, Italian-American*, etc.

LESSON 8

Smart Grammar

The verb *to be*

Use the verb *to be* to:

- introduce yourself or another person
- say where people come from

Singular

I	am (I'm)
you	are (you're)
he/she	is (he's/she's)
it	is (it's)

Examples

I'm Lisa.
He's Jake.

Activity A

Complete the sentences with the correct singular form of *to be*.

1 I ___*am*___ from England.
2 He _____ Colombian.
3 You _____ Korean.
4 She _____ from Brazil.

Plural

we	are (we're)
you	are (you're)
they	are (they're)

Examples

We're from Ecuador.
They're Irish.

Activity B

Complete the sentences with the correct plural form of *to be*.

1 You ___*are*___ American.
2 We _____ from India.
3 They _____ French.
4 Mei and Li _____ from China.

> **SMART TIP**
>
> To ask a question with *be*, place *am, are* or *is* before the subject:
>
> He is a student. → *Is he a student?*
> I am from Ireland. → *Am I from Ireland?*
> They are Filipino. → *Are they Filipino?*

Activity C

Jane, Raphaël and Paloma meet each other. Complete their conversation with the correct forms of *to be*. Add pronouns where needed.

Raphaël (to Jane) Where ___*are*___ you from?

Jane (to Raphaël and Paloma) _____ from England. _____ you Spanish?

Raphaël _____ French and Paloma _____ Mexican.

Saying Hello and Introductions   Unit 1   **13**

Activity A

Complete the table below.

Name	Country	Nationality
Pierre	France	*French*
Cassandra		Canadian
Brian	the United States	
Katie		English
Paloma	Spain	

Activity B

Use the verb *to be* to write a sentence explaining where each person is from.

1 Laura, England: _____*Laura is English.*_____

2 Carlos and Marta, Colombia: _____

3 Manmohan, India: _____

4 you, Canada: _____

5 Terre, Australia: _____

Activity C

Javier is visiting the United States. Complete his conversation with a tour guide.

Guide ___*Hello*___! Welcome to the United States!

Javier Hello! _____ Javier.
_____ your name?

Guide _____ Joe. Nice to meet you.

Javier Nice to meet you too. _____
you American?

Guide Yes. _____ from?

Javier _____ from Mexico.
_____ speak Spanish?

Guide A little.

Javier I'm sorry, my English _____ not very good.

Guide No, your English _____ very good!

Activity D

Find the names of countries and nationalities in the word search below. Be careful, they can be written horizontally, vertically or diagonally.

Australia   Canada   India   Ireland
Korea   Spain   USA

```
V  K  C  X  U  P  I  N  D  I  A  D  C  N  M  K
K  R  U  S  A  Y  J  S  J  Y  B  V  A  G  L  R
O  O  A  I  X  X  B  P  B  A  Y  M  N  R  I  J
R  S  A  U  S  T  R  A  L  I  A  N  A  Q  Ç  E
E  R  M  V  G  W  Q  I  W  E  J  T  D  A  F  Z
A  X  Z  V  G  N  D  N  I  R  E  L  A  N  D  F
P  D  V  S  U  Q  K  M  E  X  S  P  M  Z  Z  W
G  E  A  Y  A  D  B  L  S  F  Q  Z  U  Z  W  O
```

Challenge

Do you know the English word for someone from North America or South America? Write the words below.

From North America _____
From South America _____

Activity E

Find the error in each sentence. Write the corrected sentence on the line.

1 Hello! My name Laura.
*Hello! My name is Laura.*

2 We are of Canada. _____

3 John is from England. He is American. _____
_____

4 Mei is China. _____

5 I speak England. _____

6 We is from the Philippines. _____
_____

Internet Activity

Do you want to learn some names of English origin? Go to **www.berlitzpublishing.com** to find a site with first names of English origin. Try to pronounce some names. Then try to use them in the phrase *My name's… .*

Unit 2 Nouns and Numbers

In this unit you will learn:
- to identify people, animals, and things and the numbers 1-30.
- the definite article (*the*) and indefinite article (*a* and *an*).
- the simple present and the present progressive.
- to fill out a form about yourself.
- to ask for personal information about another person.

LESSON 1

A Postcard

A Postcard from New York

Read the postcard from Julien to his friend Anne. Then circle the words indicating people, things or animals.

Dear Anne,
I am having a lot of fun in New York, and I'm starting to learn a little English. Look at this (picture!) Look at the animals! Look at the cats and the dogs! Look at the people! Look at the boys, the girls, the men and the women! It's very nice here. I like the houses and buildings. Look at the cars and the taxis! They're so typical of New York! This photo shows you the people, the animals and the things that I see here. I miss you.

P.S.: What do you think of my English?
Julien

Anne Jones
299 Holloway Road
Holloway, London
N7 8HS UK

Activity A

Circle **T** for true and **F** for false.

1 Julien is on vacation in Great Britain   T / **F**
2 Julien's postcard describes mountains and rivers.   T / F
3 Julien likes the houses and buildings that he sees.   T / F
4 The postcard describes typical American things.   T / F

Activity B

Look at the postcard. Write the English words that name…

1 …people.

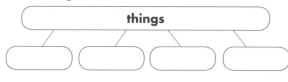

> people
> boys

2 …things.

> things

3 …animals.

> animals

Your Turn

If you know other English words for people, animals and things, add them to the spaces above.

SMART TIP

Most English words end in –s in the plural.

animal/animals	girl/girls
boy/boys	house/houses
building/buildings	taxi/taxis
car/cars	

The is the definite article for both singular and plural nouns, and *a/an* are the indefinite articles for singular nouns. *Some* is the indefinite article for plural nouns. The indefinite article *a* comes before words beginning with a consonant. *An* comes before words beginning with a vowel or a silent "h," like in *an hour*.

Essential Words

a girl   a boy   a man   a woman

a bird   a cat   a dog

a bus   a car

a street   a house   a building

Activity A
Write the English word for each item in the pictures.

1 d a *a girl* c b

2 a e b g d c f h

Activity B
Write the correct indefinite article for each word.

1 __a__ dog
2 ____ boy
3 ____ girl
4 ____ orange
5 ____ animal
6 ____ house
7 ____ American
8 ____ building

Smart Phrases

Essential Phrases

Look at the people!
Look at the animals!
Look at the people!
I miss you.

Activity A

Mary is walking with James. While they walk, she shows him people and animals. Write a sentence in each speech bubble to indicate what Mary shows to James.

1 _____
_____

2 _____
_____

Activity B

Fill in the empty spaces to help Blanca write a post card to Marta from New York.

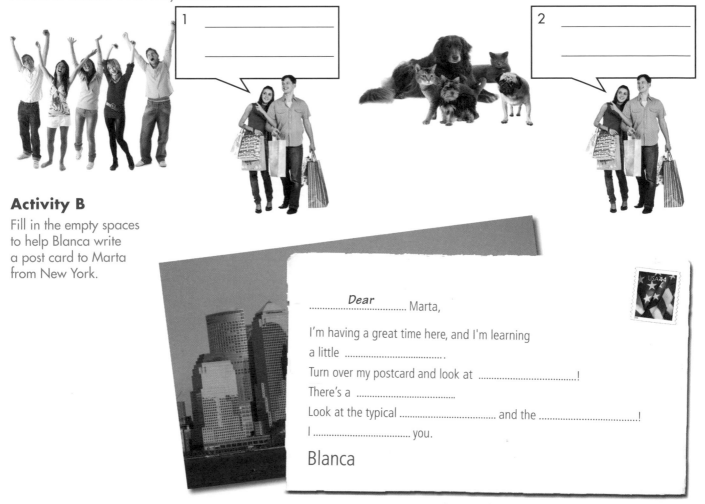

Dear .... Marta,

I'm having a great time here, and I'm learning
a little ....
Turn over my postcard and look at ....!
There's a ....
Look at the typical .... and the ....!
I .... you.

Blanca

LESSON 4

Smart Grammar

Singular and Plural Nouns

To form the plural of an English noun, add an –s in most cases: *house/houses, car/cars, toy/toys.*

There are some exceptions:

- if a word ends in –x or –ch, add –es: *box/boxes, watch/watches*
- if a word ends in a consonant + –y, replace –y with –ies: *baby/babies, cherry/cherries*
- if a word ends in –fe or –lf, its plural ending is –ves: *knife/knives, life/lives, shelf/shelves*
- some words are irregular and don't follow the typical rules: *man/men, women/women, person/people, child/children, mouse/mice*
- some nouns cannot be made plural: *luggage, information*

SMART TIP

The definite article in English is *the*. It is used to refer to a particular object or objects *(Look at the people in the postcard!)*. For generalizations, *the* is not used.

Italian food is delicious.
Cars are very practical.

SMART TIP

Use the conjunction *and* before the last item of a list:

I speak French, English and Spanish.

Activity A

Write the plural form of the following words.

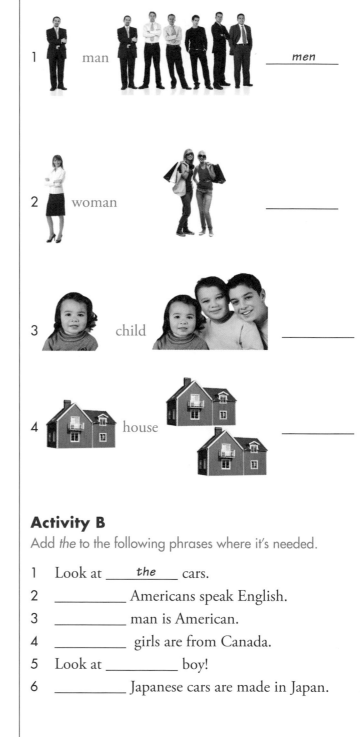

1 man   ____*men*____

2 woman   _____

3 child   _____

4 house   _____

Activity B

Add *the* to the following phrases where it's needed.

1 Look at ____*the*____ cars.

2 _____ Americans speak English.

3 _____ man is American.

4 _____ girls are from Canada.

5 Look at _____ boy!

6 _____ Japanese cars are made in Japan.

Jennifer Jameson

HOLDER / SIGNATURE DU TITULAIRE / FIRMA DEL TITULAR

UNITED STATES OF AMERICA
Type / Type / Tipo   Code / Code / Código   Passport No / No du Passeport / No. de Pasaporte
P   USA   98765234500
Surname / Nom / Apellidos
JAMESON
Given Names / Prénoms / Nombres
JENNIFER   K
Nationality / Nationalité / Nacionalidad
UNITED STATES OF AMERICA
Date of birth / Date de naissance / Fecha de nacimiento
6/30/78
Place of birth / Lieu de naissance / Lugar de nacimiento   Sex / Sexe / Sexo
27 MAIN ST AKRON OHIO 44313   **F**
Date of issue / Date de délivrance / Fecha de expedición   Authority / Autorité / Autoridad
2007   **United States**
Date of expiration / Date d'expiration / Fecha de caducidad   **Department of State**
2017
Endorsements / Mentions Spéciales / Anotaciones
SEE PAGE 27   **USA**

P<USAJAMESON<<JENNIFER<<<<<<<<<<<<<<<<<<<<<<<<<<<<<

CULTURE TIP

In the United States, dates are written as month/day/year, while in other English-speaking countries, people write the date as day/month/year. The date 06/30/2015 is written as June 30, 2015 in the U.S., and 30/06/2015 as 30 June 2015 in the United Kingdom.

Student Identification

Jennifer is an American student. She wants to study Spanish in Spain. Here is her passport.

Activity A

Answer the questions using information from Jennifer's passport.

1   What's Jennifer's last name?

   Jameson

2   What's her date of birth?

   _____

3   What's her place of birth?

   _____

4   When does she need a new passport?

   _____

Activity B

People from most countries need a Customs Card to enter the United States. Fill in this Customs Card with your own information.

U.S. Customs and Border Protection
Welcomes You to the United States

Mr./Mrs./Ms./	Last Name	First Name
	Place of Birth	Nationality
Birth Date day: month: year:		
Home Address Street & Number	City	
		Zip code
Country	Home Telephone	
U.S. Street Address (hotel name/destination)	City	State

Signature   Date

Essential Words

Numbers

0	zero	11	eleven
1	one	12	twelve
2	two	13	thirteen
3	three	14	fourteen
4	four	15	fifteen
5	five	16	sixteen
6	six	17	seventeen
7	seven	18	eighteen
8	eight	19	nineteen
9	nine	20	twenty
10	ten	30	thirty

Personal Information

avenue
address
zip code (Am.)/postcode (Brit.)
street
(tele)phone

Activity A

Fill in the missing numbers:

fifteen, sixteen, seventeen, _eighteen_ , _____,

twenty, twenty-one, twenty-two, twenty-three,

_____, _____, _____, _____,

_____, _____, thirty

CULTURE TIP

The word *name* usually means a full name, which is made up of a first name and a last name. People say *first name* (or *given name* in formal language) and *last name* or *surname* for the family name.

Activity B

Read the numbers 1 through 30 aloud. Then match each number below with its written form.

1	twelve	**4**	ten
6	one	**9**	fifteen
13	thirty	**12**	fourteen
18	six	**15**	four
10	thirteen	**22**	twenty-two
30	eighteen	**14**	nine

Activity C

Write the numbers below in their numerical form.

1   Number eleven

    _11_____

2   House number twenty-one, Harvey Street

    _____

3   Phone number seven-one-eight, three-seven-five, four-two- one-nine

    _____

4   Zip code five eight two nine six

    _____

CULTURE TIPS

- The postal code in the U.S. is a *zip code*. It is written at the end of the address and is made up of numbers. For example: 10013.

- In Great Britain, a *postcode* is made up of letters and numbers. For example: W1H 2BQ.

- In the United States, people often say "Oh" when they mean "zero," especially when giving phone numbers and zip codes: *My zip code is one-oh-oh-one-three* (10013).

Smart Phrases

Essential Phrases

What's your address?

What's your date of birth?

What's your phone number?

My address is...

My birthday is...

My phone number is...

Where do you live?

SMART TIP

To ask for someone's e-mail address, say *What's your e-mail address?* To give someone your e-mail address, say *My e-mail address is...*

Activity A

Fill in the blanks with your information.

name _____

date of birth _____

address _____

_____

phone number _____

Activity B

What does Karine ask Peter? Circle the correct answer.

1 *Where do you live?*

(a) where he lives   **b** where he works

2 *What's your address?*

a his address   **b** his phone number

3 *What's your phone number?*

a his phone number   **b** his date of birth

4 *What's your date of birth?*

a his place of birth   **b** his date of birth

LESSON 8 — Smart Grammar

The Simple Present

In English, the simple present tense talks about actions that are usually true, like routines *(I study English every day)* and actions that are always true, like facts *(People from Spain speak Spanish).*

The affirmative form is the infinitive of the verb *(to speak)* without *to*. The third person singular *(he, she, it)* is the only one that changes. The negative and question forms use *do* or *does*. *(Do you speak Chinese? Yes, I do/No, I don't).*

to speak

Affirmative	Negative	Question
I speak	I don't* speak	Do I speak?
you speak	you don't speak	Do you speak?
he/she/it speaks	he/she/it doesn't	Does he/she/it?
we speak	we don't speak	Do we speak?
you speak	you don't speak	Do you speak?
they speak	they don't speak	Do they speak?

Activity A

Conjugate the verb *to work* in the simple present affirmative, negative and question forms.

	Affirmative	Negative	Question
I	work	don't work	Do I work?
you			
he/she/it			
we			
you			
they			

SMART TIP

Only verbs that describe actions can be progressive. Verbs describing states, like *be*, cannot be progressive: *We are in Canada right now.*

The Present Progressive

The present progressive expresses an action that is taking place now. *(I am reading about verbs right now.)* It takes the helping verb *to be* and adds the ending *–ing* to the main verb.

If a verb ends in *–e (to live)*, this *–e* is replaced with *–ing (living).*

Affirmative	Negative	Question
I am working	I'm not working	Am I working?
you are working	you're not working; you aren't working*	Are you working?
he/she/it is working	he's/she's/it's not working; he/she/it isn't working	Is he/she/it working?
we are working	we're not working; we aren't working	Are we working?
you are working	you're not working; you aren't working	Are you working?
they are working	they're not working; they aren't working	Are they working?

Examples

I usually work in London.
At the moment, I'm working in Paris.

Activity B

Write the verb in parentheses in the simple present or the present progressive.

1. They usually ___*visit*___ museums in New York. (to visit)

2. At the moment she _____ English. (to speak)

3. Right now I _____. (to work)

4. You _____ English every day. (to study)

5. We always _____ to travel. (to like)

6. He _____ a book now. (to read)

Unit 2   Review

Activity A

How many can you count? Write the number and the noun. Use the correct plural form.

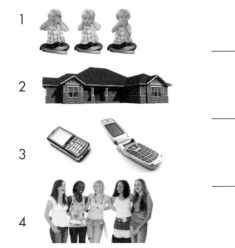

1   _three boys_

2   _____

3   _____

4   _____

Activity B

Use the information in the address book to write full sentences. Use the hints to help you.

Sally Colbert 25 Huron Street	482 913 7391
Edward Gainsbright 15 Columbia Street	+44 828 227 1984
Andrew Rodrick 8 Sixth Avenue	+44 20 2278 3625
Corrine & Mark Smith 30 Little Road	716 548 3549

1   Andrew/live

      Andrew lives at 8 Sixth Avenue.

2   Sally's phone number/be (write the number in all letters!)

   _____

3   Corrine and Mark/live

   _____

4   Andrew's phone number/be (write the number in all letters!)

   _____

5   Sally/live

   _____

Activity C

Write the correct indefinite article (a, an, some) next to each word.

1   __a__ car   3   ____ bus

2   ____ hour   4   ____ animals

Activity D

You have just arrived in the offices of the Perfect English Language School to study English. Jennifer, in the registration office, needs some information about you. Complete the conversation.

Jennifer   Hello. What's your name?

     You   _My name is... (your name here)_ _____

Jennifer   Good, what's your phone number?

     You   _____

Jennifer   What's your address?

     You   _____

Jennifer   And what's your zip code?

     You   _____

Jennifer   And last, what's your date of birth?

     You   _____

Jennifer   Excellent! Welcome to the Perfect English Language School.

     You   _____

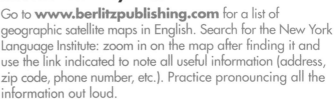

Internet Activity

Go to **www.berlitzpublishing.com** for a list of geographic satellite maps in English. Search for the New York Language Institute: zoom in on the map after finding it and use the link indicated to note all useful information (address, zip code, phone number, etc.). Practice pronouncing all the information out loud.

Unit 3 Time and Date

In this unit you will learn:
- to say the time and the date.
- the numbers from 31.
- to ask questions with *what, when* and *how long*.
- more English verbs.

LESSON 1

What time is it?

Dialogue

Diana and Joe are watching a basketball game. Listen to their conversation.

Diana What time is it?

Joe It's half past six.

Diana It's early! When does the game end?

Joe In twenty-five minutes.

Diana How long does it last?

Joe It lasts forty-eight minutes.

Diana What's the score?

Joe Knicks 48, Bulls 42.

Activity A

Look at the dialogue again and answer the questions below.

1 What time is it?
   It's half past six.

2 When does the game end?

3 How long does it last?

4 What's the score?

Activity B

Put the dialogue in order.
Number the phrases 1–4.

CULTURE TIP

In Great Britain and in the United States, people mostly use the 12-hour clock (from 1 to 12) to give the time. 18:35 is *6:35 PM* (six thirty-five PM). To tell if someone is talking about time in the morning or in the afternoon, add the abbreviation AM for times between midnight and noon. For times between noon and midnight, add the abbreviation PM. In general, simply say *It's one o'clock, It's two o'clock* when the time of day is clear.

Smart Phrases

Essential Phrases

What time is it?

How long does it last?

When does it end?

It's one a.m.   `AM 1:00`

It's two a.m.   `AM 2:00`

It's two p.m.   `PM 2:00`

It's ten p.m.   `PM 10:00`

It's seven thirty./It's half past seven.   `AM PM 7:30`

It's a quarter after/past six.   `AM PM 6:15`

It's a quarter to seven.   `AM PM 6:45`

It's late!

It's early!

Activity A

You have an appointment with a friend at 8:00 PM. For each of the times below, say if it is late or early for your appointment time.

1   It's six forty five.   _It's early!_

2   It's a quarter past eight. _____

3   It's seven thirty. _____

4   It's nine o'clock. _____

Activity B

Look at the clock and write a sentence telling what time it is.

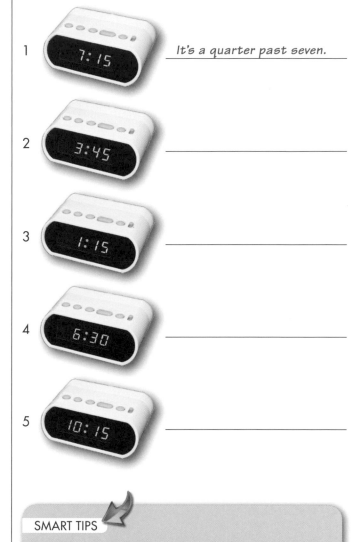

1   7:15   _It's a quarter past seven._

2   3:45   _____

3   1:15   _____

4   6:30   _____

5   10:15   _____

SMART TIPS

- There is more than one way to say the time in English: *It's twenty to eight = It's seven forty. It's ten to five = It's four fifty.* Time can also be read the way it appears on digital clocks: *it's 7:20 (it's seven twenty), it's 4:15 (it's four fifteen), it's 9:35 (it's nine thirty-five).*

- When telling time in English, *half* means *thirty minutes* and *a quarter* means *fifteen minutes*.

  It's seven thirty (Am.) = It's half past seven (Brit.) = It's thirty minutes after seven.

  It's six fifteen. = It's a quarter past six. = It's fifteen minutes after six.

Words to Know

Essential Words

Time

an hour

a minute

a second

at ... o'clock

Numbers

31	thirty-one
32	thirty-two
33	thirty-three
34	thirty-four
35	thirty-five
40	forty
50	fifty
60	sixty
70	seventy
80	eighty
90	ninety
100	one hundred
101	one hundred and one
102	one hundred and two

Extra Words

half

quarter

> **SMART TIP**
>
> Have you noticed how the numbers 31 through 35 are formed? The numbers between tens (30, 40, 50, etc.) always follow the same model with a hyphen: *thirty-one, thirty-two,* etc. After 100, they sometimes appear after the word *and*: 101 = *one hundred (and) one,* 125 = *one hundred (and) twenty-five.* Do you know how to say the numbers 36 through 40?

Activity A

Write out the following numbers in letters.

1 44 *forty-four* _____

2 32 _____

3 67 _____

4 58 _____

Activity B

When does the show end? The show starts at eight PM and ends at ten PM. Look at the times below and write how long it is until the show ends. Write it out in letters.

1 `8:45 PM` *It ends in one hour and fifteen minutes.*

_____

2 `8:00 PM` _____

_____

3 `9:55 PM` _____

_____

4 `8:15 PM` _____

_____

5 `9:30 PM` _____

_____

Your Turn

What time do you usually do the following activities?

wake up *I usually wake up at...*

eat breakfast _____

go to work or school _____

go to bed _____

LESSON 4
Smart Grammar

Prepositions of Movement and Location

Prepositions are words that describe a location or a movement.

Prepositions of Location

Prepositions of location show the place where someone or something is located.

behind/in back of

in front of

on

over

between

next to

under

Examples   The cat is sitting on the desk.
The ball is under the table.
The tree is in front of the house.

Prepositions of Movement

Prepositions of movement show the direction where someone or something is moving. Prepositions of movement are used with verbs of motion.

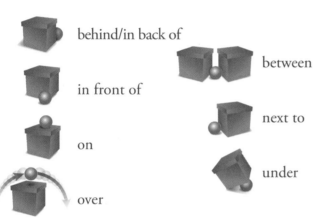

across

away from

into

out of

around

down

off

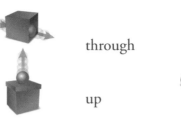

through

up

past

towards

Examples   The man is walking across the bridge.
I'm walking up the stairs.
She's walking down the stairs.
The ball is falling off the box.

Activity A

Write the preposition that describes the location of the ball.

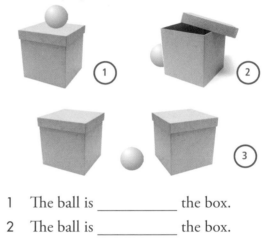

1   The ball is _____ the box.
2   The ball is _____ the box.
3   The ball is _____ the boxes.

Activity B

Write the preposition that describes the movement of the ball.

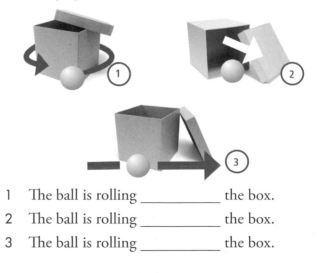

1   The ball is rolling _____ the box.
2   The ball is rolling _____ the box.
3   The ball is rolling _____ the box.

LESSON 5
Things to do

do the laundry

do my homework

sweep the floor

call Mary

exercise (Am.) /
do exercises (Brit.)

Julia's To-Do List

Julia is thinking about what she has to do today.
Look at the pictures and her to-do list.

Activity A

Choose the correct answer.

1   What does Julia have to do first?
    (a) do the laundry   **b   do her homework**

2   What word is associated with the verb "to sweep"?
    a   clothes   **b   floor**

3   What expression means "to do work for school"?
    a   do my homework   **b   exercise**

4   What will Julia do before calling Mary?
    a   exercise   **b   do her homework**

To do
do the laundry
sweep the floor
do my homework
call Mary
exercise

Activity B

Write what Julia has to do today according to the pictures.

1   *Julia has to do her homework.*

3   _____

Carlos
718-829-0323

2   _____

4   _____

LESSON 6

Words to Know

Essential Words

Days of the Week

Sunday
Monday
Tuesday
Wednesday
Thursday
Friday
Saturday

Months of the Year

January
February
March
April
May
June
July
August
September
October
November
December

SMART TIPS

- In English, the days of the week and the months of the year are all written with a capital letter at the beginning of the word.

- The year is read in two parts: the first two digits, then the last two. For example, 1998 is *nineteen ninety-eight*; 2015 is *twenty fifteen* or *two thousand fifteen*.

- The date often takes a *–th* ending after the digits, except for the numbers 1, 2, and 3 (4th, 5th, 6th, etc., or *fourth, fifth, sixth*, etc.). 1 takes *–st* (1st, *first*), 2 takes *–nd* (2nd, *second*), and 3 takes *–rd* (3rd, *third*). These abbreviations are also found in compound numbers: 21st, 22nd, 23rd.

Activity A

Look at Kevin's schedule for the week. Answer the questions below.

DIARY	
Monday	exercise
Tuesday	sweep the floor
Wednesday	do my homework
Thursday	exercise
Friday	call my parents
Saturday	do my homework
Sunday	do the laundry

1   What day does Kevin sweep his house? __Tuesday__

2   What days does Kevin exercise? _____ and _____

3   What day does Kevin call his parents? _____

4   What days does Kevin do his homework? _____ and _____

5   What day does Kevin do the laundry? _____

Activity B

Write each date in English.

1   Thursday 2/24   ___Thursday, February 24th___

2   Monday 11/17   _____

3   Saturday 6/5   _____

4   Wednesday 9/21   _____

5   Friday 4/3   _____

6   Tuesday 1/31   _____

7   Sunday 10/12   _____

8   Thursday 3/25   _____

9   Sunday 8/22   _____

Smart Phrases

Essential Phrases

What day is today?
Today is Tuesday.
What's the date today?
What month is it?
What year is it?

Activity A

Circle the correct answer.

1   What day is today?
   a   January   (**b**)   **Tuesday**

2   What month is it?
   a   Monday   **b   December**

3   What's the date today?
   a   Today is July 14, 2012.   **b   Today is Wednesday.**

4   What year is it?
   a   August 23rd   **b   2015**

Activity B

Write the questions to complete the mini-dialogues.

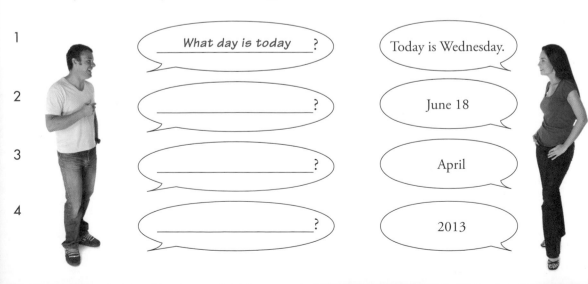

1   _What day is today_ ?   Today is Wednesday.

2   _____ ?   June 18

3   _____ ?   April

4   _____ ?   2013

LESSON 8

Smart Grammar

The verbs *to do* and *to make*

The verbs *to do* and *to make* are very useful, common verbs in English. It is important for you to know the difference between the two.

In general, *to make* means to create something.

In general, *to do* means to perform an action.

Examples

to do:
to do homework
to do housework
to do the dishes
to do the laundry

to make:
to make a cake
to make the bed
to make tea
to make a phone call
to make a mistake
to make a decision

CULTURE TIPS

American and British English sometimes use different expressions to talk about the same thing. For example, Americans *do the dishes*, while in the UK, *people do the washing up*. Americans also *do the laundry*, while in the UK people *do the washing*.

Activity A

What are they doing? Match each picture with the phrase that describes what the person is doing.

1   He is making coffee. _____
2   They are making a decision. _____
3   She is making a cake. _____

Activity B

Complete the following sentences with *to do* or *to make* in the present progressive.

1   a cake: he _____ *He is making a cake.* _____

2   the gardening: Lucio _____

3   the laundry: Sheila _____

4   a decision: Jan and Betty _____

5   tea: Isabella _____

6   the bed: Li _____

7   homework: Abdul and Badra _____

8   a phone call: Cynthia _____

9   the dishes: Khanh _____

10 housework: Paul _____

11 a mistake: Janis _____

Your Turn

Write sentences (in the simple present) about your favorite weekend activities. Don't forget to use the verbs *to do/to make*.

On Saturdays I do the housework and I cook.

I also _____

_____

_____

_____

_____

_____

Activity A

Use the activities below to say what Sara does at each time of the day. Start your sentences with *She*.

> sweep the floor   exercise   do her homework
> call Julia   do the laundry

1 *PM 12:30*

   She does her homework at twelve thirty.

2 *PM 8:45*

   _____

3 *PM 6:00*

   _____

4 *AM 7:45*

   _____

5 *AM 11:15*

   _____

Activity B

Look at the times. Say how long the game will take to finish.

1 1:31:02   *It ends in one hour, thirty-one minutes and two seconds.*

2 2:34:13   _____

3 0:0:27   _____

4 0:12:39   _____

Activity C

Emily lost her planner and forgot what she has to do in February. Look at the calendar and answer the questions.

FEBRUARY						
Monday	Tuesday	Wednesday	Thursday	Friday	Saturday	Sunday
1	2	3 do the laundry	4	5	6	7
8	9	10	11	12	13 do some housework	14
15 call Philip	16	17	18 do some shopping	19	20	21 do some cooking
22	23 wash the car	24	25	26	27	28

What are the dates Emily planned to do these activities? Write the date in the order day/month/date.

1 wash the car

   Tuesday, February 23rd

2 do the laundry

   _____

3 do some shopping

   _____

4 do some housework

   _____

5 call Philip

   _____

> ### Challenge
> Write a paragraph about a friend. Tell what he or she does regularly during the week.

Internet Activity

Do you want to take a vacation to the British Isles or the United States? **www.berlitzpublishing.com** for a list of sites to help you plan your trip. Use your knowledge about dates and times to find the best price and quality. How much does it cost to arrive at 10:00 a.m. on a Saturday morning? And to return on a Sunday evening?

Unit 4 Family

In this unit you will learn:

- to introduce your family and talk about your relatives.
- to use *there is* and *there are*.
- to use possessive adjectives and demonstrative pronouns in English.
- the differences between *a/an, any* and *some*.
- the forms of *to have* in American English and British English.

LESSON 1 Family Photo

Clare and her parents

Steve

Mick and Monica

Patricia

Dialogue

Clare and Sam are talking about their families. Clare is showing Sam a picture of each member of her family.

Clare Look at this photo of my family, Sam. I have two brothers and one sister.

Sam What a big family! This is you, and those are your parents, I think?

Clare Yes, that's my mother and that's my father. Look at this photo. This is my younger sister, Patricia.

Sam And those are your brothers?

Clare Yes. This is my older brother, Mick. And that's my younger brother, Steve.

Sam And who's that?

Clare That's Monica, Mick's wife.

Activity A

Circle **T** for true or **F** for false.

1 There are four people in Clare's family.   T/**F**
2 Patricia is Clare's sister.   T/F
3 Clare has three brothers.   T/F
4 Monica is Clare's mother.   T/F

Activity B

Circle the picture that describes each sentence.

1 This is my father.   **a** / b

2 This is my sister.   a / b

3 This is my mother.   a / b

4 These are my brothers.   a / b

5 This is Mick's wife.   a / b

SMART TIPS

- *There is* is used for the singular (one) and *there are* is used for the plural (more than one) person, animal or thing. For example: *There is a dog in the house. There are three men in the street.*

- To form the negative add *not* after the verb: *there is not…* (*there isn't/there's not…*) and *there are not…* (*there aren't…*). For example: *There isn't/There's not a dog in the house. There aren't any brothers in Paco's family.*

- To ask a question use *Is there…?* or *Are there…?* For example: *Is there a cat in the postcard? Are there a lot of people in your family?*

Words to Know

Essential Words

family
parents
father
mother
children
son
daughter
brother
sister
husband
wife

older
younger
I think…
What a big family!

Sam's Family Tree

Thomas   Marianne

Sam   Rachel   Paul

There are two ways to express possession in English:
- by using possessive adjectives such as *my*. They will be presented in Lesson 4.
- by adding an apostrophe + *s* (*'s*) to a name:
  Marianne's husband = the husband of Marianne.
  Steve's brother = the brother of Steve. In the plural add only an apostrophe: *My parents' house* = the house of my parents.

Activity A

Look at Sam's Family Tree. Complete his description below.

1 There are five people in my __family__ .

2 Thomas is my _____ .

3 My _____ 's name is Marianne.

4 Rachel is my _____ .

5 Paul is Rachel's _____ .

Activity B

Circle the correct word.

1 Sam is Rachel's (**brother**) **father**.

2 Rachel is Sam's **mother** **sister**.

3 Marianne is Sam's **father** **mother**.

4 Thomas is his **uncle** **father**.

5 Marianne and Thomas are Sam and Rachel's **parents** **brothers**.

6 Sam is Thomas and Marianne's **son** **daughter**.

7 Rachel is Thomas and Marianne's **sister** **daughter**.

8 Sam and Rachel are Thomas and Marianne's **children** **parents**.

9 Rachel is Paul's **wife** **sister**.

10 Paul is Rachel's **father** **husband**.

Smart Phrases

Essential Phrases

Do you have (Am.)/Have you got (Brit.) a big family?
I have (Am.)/I've got (Brit.) two brothers and one sister.
My family is big/small.
What a big/small family!

Activity A

Put the sentences in the correct order to create a dialogue.

Do you have a big family?

1

What a big family!

#

No, My family is small. I just have one sister.

#

I've got three brothers and two sisters. Look at this photo.

#

Yes, I have a big family. And do you have a big family?

#

Activity B

Write a sentence saying if the families are big or small.

1   *It's a small family.*

2   _____

3   _____

4   _____

Your Turn

Use the vocabulary and the phrases you just learned to talk about your family. Is it a big or small family? Do you have any brothers or sisters? If yes, how many?

Smart Grammar

Possessive Adjectives

In Lesson 2 we learned to use 's to express possession (ownership) (*Rachel is Sam's sister*). A second way to express possession is with possessive adjectives:

my
your (sing.)
his (m.)/her (f.)/its
our
your (pl.)
their

Examples

Rachel is *his* sister.
He is *my* brother.
They are *your* sisters.
Her family is big.
Our mother's name is Karen.

Activity A

Using the pronouns in parentheses, fill in the blanks with the correct possessive adjective.

1   She is ___my___ mother.   (me)

2   Is she _____ sister?   (you)

3   _____ family is small.   (they)

4   This is _____ brother.   (me)

5   Are they _____ cousins?   (you)

6   These men are _____ brothers.   (she)

7   _____ house is big.   (he)

8   These are _____ children.   (we)

Demonstrative Adjectives

This describes a person, animal or thing that is physically close to the person who is speaking. The plural of *this* is *these*.

Examples

This man is my husband.   These people are my sisters.

That is used for a person, animal or thing that is physically far from the person who is speaking. The plural of *that* is *those*.

Examples

That is my husband.   Those are my sisters.

Activity B

Match the pictures with the correct sentences.

1   These girls are my daughters.   ___e___

2   This car is new.   _____

3   That house is big.   _____

4   This woman is my mother.   _____

5   These people are my parents.   _____

6   Those dogs like to play.   _____

SMART TIP

Possessive adjectives come before nouns. Possessive pronouns replace possessive adjectives + nouns. (*my sister = mine, their sister = theirs*).

mine   ours
yours (sing.)   yours (pl.)
his/hers/its   theirs

This is your house and that is *mine*. = This is your house and that is *my house*.

These are my brothers and those are *yours*. = These are my brothers and those are *your brothers*.

Family Tree

Pamela Johnson just created her family tree to explain who's who in her family. Look at the tree and say out loud what the relationship is between each of the family members.

Activity A

Describe the relationship between each person and Pamela.

1   Bill is Pamela's ___grandfather___ .

2   Lucy and Chris are Pamela's

    _____ .

3   Alice is Pamela's _____ .

4   Jacky is Pamela's _____ .

Activity B

How is each person related to Pamela?

1   ___mother___

2   _____

3   _____

4   _____

Ellen
(grandmother)

Bill
(grandfather)

Kate
(aunt)

Tim
(uncle)

Lucy
(mother)

Chris
(father)

Grant
(cousin)

Alice
(cousin)

Pamela

Luke
(brother)

Nadia
(sister-in-law)

Jake
(nephew)

Jacky
(niece)

SMART TIP

The prefix step- is used for relatives by remarriage: *step-father, step-sister,* etc.

My mother has a new husband, so now I have a step-father.

LESSON 6
Words to Know

Essential Words

grandfather
grandmother
grandchildren
grandson
granddaughter
uncle
aunt
nephew
niece
cousin
friend
boyfriend
girlfriend

father-in-law
mother-in-law
brother-in-law
sister-in-law
son-in-law
daughter-in-law

SMART TIP

The ending *-in-law* is used for relatives by marriage: *mother-in-law, father-in-law, sister-in-law, brother-in-law, son-in-law, daughter-in-law.*

Activity A

Look at Pamela's family tree on page 39. Circle **T** for true and **F** for false.

1 Ellen is Pamela's grandmother.   **T**/F
2 Pamela is Lucy's mother.   T/F
3 Kate is Pamela's uncle.   T/F
4 Jake is Pamela's nephew.   T/F

Activity B

Circle the words that describe the relationships.

1 My mother's sister is my…
   (a) aunt   b cousin

2 My aunt's son is my…
   a nephew   b cousin

3 My father's mother is my…
   a aunt   b grandmother

4 My brother's cousin is my…
   a cousin   b nephew

5 My father's father is my…
   a uncle   b grandfather

6 My father's niece is my…
   a sister   b cousin

SMART TIP

The word *love* is often used to talk both about what you really like to eat, drink, etc. as well as people who you love: *I love chocolate! I love my parents.*

Smart Phrases

Essential Phrases

Do you have (Am.)/Have you got (Brit.) any relatives in…?
Is your family close?
My family is close.
Are you married?
I'm single.
I love my family.
I love you.

SMART TIP

To ask a yes/no question with regular verbs, start with *do* or *does*, followed by the subject, followed by the main verb:

do/does + subject + main verb

*Do you have a big family? Yes, I do./No, I don't.
Does Fatima live in Rio de Janeiro? Yes, she does./
No, she doesn't.*

1 Have you got any family in England?

2. Your brother is very nice. Is he single?

3. Do you like your brother's wife?

4. Are you married?

5. Do you have any sisters?

(a) No, he's not. He's married. This is his wife.

(b) No, I'm not. I'm single.

(c) Yes, I do. I like her very much.

(d) Yes, I have. My uncle lives in London.

(e) No, I don't, but I have two brothers.

SMART TIPS

• You can express that you like someone or something very much by using *a lot* or *very much* with the verb *to like*: *Do you like chocolate? Yes, I like it a lot.* or *I like it very much.*

• Pronouns are placed in the same place as nouns: *I love my wife./I love her.*

• We learned in Unit 2 that *some* is used with plural nouns. *Some* becomes *any* in negative statements and in questions. For example: *Miguel doesn't have any sisters. Do you have any children?*

Activity B

Write questions for the answers. Be sure to use *any*.

1 *Do you have any cousins?*

Yes, I have three cousins.

2 _____

No, I don't have any uncles.

3 _____

No, I don't have any nephews.

4 _____

Yes, I have one brother.

Your Turn

Now talk about your family members. Are you single or married? Who is married in your family? Who is single?

Smart Grammar

The verb *to have*

The verb *to have* is irregular.

I have
you have
he/she/it has
we have
you have
they have

Examples

I have two sisters.
Chen-Hsuan has three brothers.

> **SMART TIP**
>
> American English uses *to have*, but British English uses *to have got*. *To have got* is often contracted: *I have got two sisters = I've got two sisters. Clare has got one sister = Clare's got one sister.*
>
> To ask a question use *Have you got…?*, *Has he got…?*, etc.

Activity A

Circle the correct answer.

1 He _____ a cousin.

   a have   (**b**) **has**

2 You _____ a sister.

   a have   **b has**

3 I _____ an aunt.

   a have   **b has**

4 She _____ two cousins.

   a have   **b has**

5 They _____ three nieces.

   a have   **b has**

Activity B

Write sentences using the information given below. Use *have* or *has* and the correct indefinite article: *a, an* or *some.*

1 ___*He has an uncle.*___   (he, uncle)

2 _____   (my uncle, nieces)

3 _____   (I, sister-in-law)

4 _____   (she, brothers)

Your Turn

Answer the following questions about your family.

1 Do you have any sisters? _____

2 Do you have any brothers? _____

3 Do you have any aunts? _____

4 Do you have any cousins? _____

5 Do you have any pets? _____

> **CULTURE TIP**
>
>
>
> The word *woman* (pl. *women*) is used for women in general, but when you want to talk about someone in particular or about a group of women, it is more polite in British English to use the word *lady* (pl. *ladies*). For example: *These ladies are from London.*

> **SMART TIP**
>
> In addition to describing ownership and relationships (*I have two brothers*), *to have* is used in common expressions:
>
> *to have a sandwich* = to eat a sandwich
>
> *to have coffee* = to drink coffee
>
> *to have a good time* = to have fun
>
> *to have a bad time* = to not have fun

Activity A

Janet brings her friend Paul to a family party and introduces him to her relatives. Complete their conversation.

Janet That's my _grandfather_, Alfie.
         mother's father

         And that's my _____ Diane.
                       mother's mother

Paul And who is that girl?

Janet That's my _____, Penelope, and that's
         mother's niece

         my _____, Mike.
            mother's nephew

Paul Is that lady your mother?

Janet No, she's my _____, Connie.
         mother's sister

         Penelope and Mike are her _____.
                                  husband's children

Paul Who's that woman?

Janet She's Linda, my _____.
                        father's wife

Activity B

Indicate the relationship between Janet and each person, making sure to use the correct possessive adjective:

1 Connie is _____her aunt_____ .

2 Linda is _____.

3 Penelope and Mike are _____.

4 Alfie and Diane are _____.

> ### Challenge
> Ask an English-speaking friend about his or her family. Does he or she have brothers and sisters? A lot of cousins? Any nieces or nephews?

Activity C

Now Paul is asking Alfie questions about his family. Fill in the blanks with the correct demonstrative adjectives. You can use either *this* and *that* (both are correct) with singular nouns and either *these* or *those* (both are correct) with plural nouns.

Paul Is __this/that__ boy your nephew?

Alfie No, he's my grandson.

Paul Who are _____ children?

Alfie They are my grandchildren.

Paul Is _____ man your son?

Alfie No, he's my nephew! _____ men are my sons.

Activity D

Write a sentence saying how many children there are. Start each sentence with the expression *there is…* or *there are….*

1

There are two children.

2

_____

3

_____

4

_____

Internet Activity

Go to **www.berlitzpublishing.com** for a list of sites where you can create your own family tree. Create your family tree and point out each family member in English. Practice introducing them out loud in English.

Unit 5 Meals

In this unit you will learn:

- to talk about breakfast, lunch and dinner.
- vocabulary related to food and drink.
- the different uses of the verbs *to be* and *to have*.

- to ask questions in English.
- the phrases *to want* and *would like*.
- modal verbs (*can, could, may, will would*).

LESSON

1

I'm hungry!

Dialogue

Min-ji and her friend Bae are talking about what they want to eat. Listen to them talk about what they want to eat for breakfast, lunch and dinner.

Min-ji I'm hungry. Do you want some breakfast?

Bae Yes. I'd like a big salad.

Min-ji At eight o'clock in the morning? We eat salad for lunch or for dinner.

Bae I don't mind. What would you like?

Min-ji Eggs. Would you like some eggs?

Bae And I'd like a glass of wine too!

Min-ji We don't drink wine for breakfast!

Activity A

Circle **T** for true and **F** for false.

1 Min-ji wants to have breakfast. **T**/**F**
2 Bae wants to have a salad for breakfast. **T/F**
3 Min-ji tells Bae to have soup. **T/F**
4 Bae wants a glass of beer. **T/F**

Activity B

Circle the correct answer.

1 What does Min-ji want to eat? **ⓐ** **b**

2 What does Bae want to drink? **a** **b**

3 What are they going to have for breakfast? **a** **b**

4 What time does the dialogue take place? **a** **b**

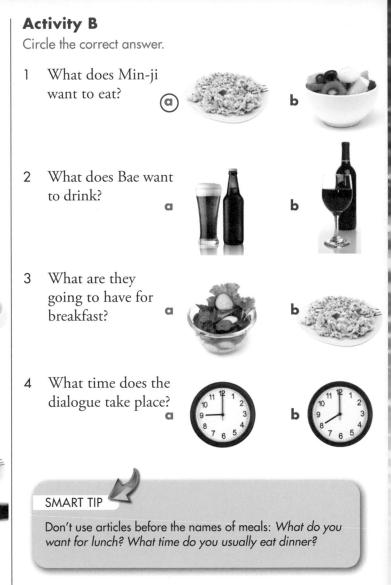

> **SMART TIP**
>
> Don't use articles before the names of meals: *What do you want for lunch? What time do you usually eat dinner?*

Words to Know

Essential Words

Food

bread

fruit

soup

Drinks

beer

coffee

juice

milk

tea

water

Verbs used for food and drinks

to drink

to eat

to have

> **SMART TIP**
>
> *Food, bread, fruit, soup, beer, coffee, juice, milk, tea* and *water* are noncount (uncountable) nouns in English. They cannot be counted, so they cannot be plural. Noncount nouns do not take singular indefinite articles (*a, an*): *water, bread, tea.* To count these items, use measure words: *a loaf of bread, two loaves of bread, a cup of tea, three cups of tea.*
>
> See page XXX for a list of noncount nouns.

> **SMART TIP**
>
> If you don't want to eat or drink something, simply say *No, thank you.*

Activity A

Look at the pictures and write the food or drink that each person is having.

1 ___fruit___   2 _____

3 _____   4 _____

> **SMART TIP**
>
> Beverages are usually noncount, but sometimes *a* or *an* describes the container a drink is in: *I'd like a coffee.* = *I'd like a cup of coffee.* Sometimes *a* or *an* describes a type (kind) of a beverage: *I tried a new beer last night.* = *I tried a new type of beer.*

Your Turn

What kinds of food do you like? List your favorite breakfast, lunch and dinner foods. Use a dictionary to look up words that you don't know in English.

1 breakfast _____

2 lunch _____

3 dinner _____

Smart Phrases

Essential Phrases

I'd like… (Am.)/I fancy… (Brit.)

I'm hungry.

I'm thirsty.

CULTURE TIP

I would (I'd) like… in American English and *I fancy…* in British English express that a person wants something. They are often used when people order food in a restaurant: *I'd like eggs and coffee, please.*

SMART TIP

The verb *to be* expresses how someone feels and is followed by an adjective. *To have* expresses possession and is followed by a noun. For example:

*I'm hungry. Ann's cold. Fynn and Leah are thirsty.
I have a white car. Sam has one sister.*

Activity A

Six people want to eat or drink different things. Check the correct box to say if the person is hungry or thirsty.

		I'm hungry.	I'm thirsty.
1	bread	✓	☐
2	coffee	☐	☐
3	soup and salad	☐	☐
4	beer and water	☐	☐
5	eggs	☐	☐
6	juice	☐	☐

Activity B

Fill in the blanks with either *I'd like* or *I fancy.*

1 _____*I'd like*_____ a salad. (American English)

2 _____ orange juice. (British English)

3 _____ soup and a salad. (British English)

4 _____ coffee. (American English)

Activity C

Put each word next to the picture it describes.

> dinner   breakfast   lunch

_____

_____

_____

Smart Grammar

Question Words

How?	How do you get to work? I walk.
What?	What do you do? I'm a teacher.
When?	When do you study English? At night.
Where?	Where do you live? In Beijing.
Which?	Which city do you live in, Beijing or Shanghai? Beijiing.
Who?	Who do you live with? My parents.
Why?	Why do you study at night? Because I work during the day.

To ask a question, start with the question word, followed by *do* or *does*, followed by the subject, followed by a main verb:

question word + *do/does* + subject + verb

When do we eat?
Where do you live?
What does she like for lunch?

Activity A

Fill in the blanks with the correct question word.

> Who   Where   When   Which   What

1   _____Where_____ do you live?
2   _____ do you like to eat for breakfast?
3   _____ does it start?
4   _____ do you like better, London or Paris?
5   _____ is that man?

Questions with *to be*

To ask a question with the verb *to be*, start with the question word, followed by *am* or *is* or *are*, followed by the subject:

question word + *am/is/are* + subject

Which is your car, the red one or the blue one?
  The blue one.
Who is she? My sister.
Where are your friends? At school.

Activity B

Choose the correct question word.

1   _____ time is it?
   ⓐ **What**   b **When**   c **Where**
2   _____ are they living now?
   a **Who**   b **Where**   c **Which**
3   _____ is the capital of France?
   a **What**   b **How**   c **Why**
4   _____ is Lisa's favorite color, yellow or green?
   a **Which**   b **Where**   c **When**

Activity C

What question word do you use to ask…

1   …the reason for something?
   _____Why_____
2   …the identity of someone?
   _____
3   …what time something happens?
   _____
4   …the place someone is from?
   _____

Your Turn

Read the following answers. Then ask a question related to each answer. Practice saying the questions and answers aloud.

1   My mother's name is Mary. *What's your mother's name?*
2   It's three PM.
3   They're Jane's cousins.
4   She lives in London.

At the restaurant

Menu

Read the menu aloud. Then, listen to the dialogue between Marta and the waiter.

Good Food Restaurant

Menu
Appetizers

Shrimp cocktail
Soup

Main course

Burger and fries
Chicken with rice
Fish with vegetables

Dessert

Chocolate cake

Ice cream

Dialogue

Waiter Hello. Would you like a starter?

Marta Yes, I'll have a shrimp cocktail for the appetizer, please.

Waiter Fine. What would you like for the main course?

Marta What do you recommend?

Waiter The burger is delicious.

Marta I don't want meat. I don't like it.

Waiter The fish and vegetables are also very good.

Marta OK. I'll have the fish and vegetables.

Waiter Fine. That's a good choice. I'll bring it right away.

Activity A

Circle the correct answer.

1   What appetizer does Marta order?

2   What food does the waiter suggest but Marta doesn't want?

3   What does Marta order as a main course?

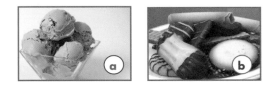

4   What dessert is on the menu?

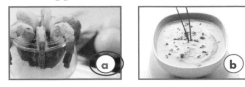

Activity B

Put the sentences in the correct order to create a dialogue.

____   I'll have the soup for an appetizer, please.

____   And for the main course?

_1_   What would you like for an appetizer?

____   I'll have the chicken.

> **CULTURE TIP**
>
> The first course is called the *starter* in British English and the *appetizer* in American English. *Prawn cocktail* in British English is called *shrimp cocktail* in American English. Also, it is much easier to find the traditional *fish and chips* on a British menu, not the American *burger and fries*!
>
> Potato chips are called *crisps* in Great Britain and *chips* in the United States. Fries are called *chips* in Great Britain while they're called *fries* or *French fries* in the United States.

Words to Know

Essential Words

apple pie
cake
cheese
chicken
fish
ice cream
meat
pepper
potatoes
rice
salad
salt
vegetables

Activity A

Write whether the following dishes are served as an appetizer, main course or dessert.

1   soup and shrimp cocktail _____

2   meat and fish _____

3   ice cream and apple pie _____

4   chicken and rice _____

CULTURE TIP

In Great Britain and in the United States, it is customary to leave a tip for the server, generally 15% of the total bill in the United States and 10% in Great Britain.

Activity B

Answer the questions. Write complete sentences.

1   Which is an appetizer/a starter?

_____

2   Which is a main course?

_____

3   Which is a dessert?

_____

Your Turn

Use your new vocabulary and sentences to create your own menu.

Restaurant_____

Menu
Appetizers
_____
_____

Main course
_____
_____

Dessert
_____
_____

Drinks
_____
_____

LESSON 7

Smart Phrases

Essential Phrases

Can I see the wine list?

What's today's special?

The special is…

Enjoy your meal.

How is your food?

This is delicious!

Could I have the check (Am.)/bill (Brit.)/, please?

It's on me.

Activity A

What do you say when you want to…

1   …wish someone a pleasant meal?

Enjoy your meal.

2   …ask the waiter for the bill?

3   …ask for the wine list?

4   …say that your food tastes really good?

Activity B

Circle the best response to the questions and situations below.

1   What's today's special?

   a   It's delicious.

   ⓑ   The special today is the fish.

2   Before beginning the meal, you want to drink something. You say to the waiter:

   a   Could I see the wine menu, please?

   b   Enjoy your meal.

3   You are eating and the server asks you if you are enjoying your meal. Your answer is:

   a   The special is the fish.

   b   It's delicious!

4   You have finished your meal. You say to the waiter:

   a   Could I have the bill, please?

   b   What's the special today?

Your Turn

You're in a restaurant with a friend. Describe to him or her the different dishes, the menu and today's specials. Ask your friend what he or she wants to eat. At the end, make sure you pay your bill!

LESSON 8
Smart Grammar

Modal Verbs

Certain verbs in English, called modal verbs (modals), are used together with main verbs. Common modals are *can, could, may, will* and *would.* Main verbs follow modals and use the infinitive.

- The modals *can, could, will* and *would* make requests (ask somebody to do something for you). Adding *please* makes the request more polite:

Can you tell us about today's specials, please?

Could you please bring the wine list?

Will you please bring me a glass of wine?

Would you please bring the check?

- The modals *can, could* and *may* ask permission (ask somebody if it's okay for you to do something):

Can I have fish with vegetables, please?

Could we please order now?

May I see the wine list?

CULTURE TIP

To ask for something politely in English, expressions like *I'd like,* the abbreviated form of *I would like,* or *I'll have,* the abbreviated form of *I will have,* are much more polite than *I want.*

Activity A
Circle the correct modal.

1 _____ I have some wine, please?

   ⓐ Can   **b Will**

2 _____ you please bring us a menu?

   a May   **b Would**

3 _____ you tell us about the desserts?

   a Could   **b May**

4 _____ we have the check?

   a May   **b Would**

Activity B
Are *can* and *could* used for requests or permission?

1 Can I please have a cup of coffee?

   permission

2 Could you tell us about the appetizers?

   _____

3 Can you bring us the bill?

   _____

4 Could we see the wine list, please?

   _____

Your Turn
You're in a restaurant. Think of questions to ask the waiter.

1 Can _____?

2 May _____?

3 Will _____?

4 Would _____?

5 Could _____?

Activity A

Use the verb *to be* or *to have* to complete the sentences.

1 He _____has_____ brown eyes.

1 She _____ hungry.

3 They _____ tall.

4 We _____ thirsty.

5 You _____ blond hair.

6 My parents _____ a new car.

7 He _____ cold.

8 You _____ happy!

Activity B

The dishes have all been mixed up on the Eat Out Restaurant menu. Someone put desserts where the appetizers should be and main courses after the desserts! Cross out the mistakes and replace them with the correct words.

EAT OUT RESTAURANT
Menu

Appetizers
~~Apple pie~~ Soup
Chicken with rice

Main course
Chocolate cake
Shrimp cocktail

Dessert
Soup
Burger and fries

Activity C

Bill is hungry. He invites Angela to go out to eat with him. Use the phrases and question words learned in this unit to fill in the blanks in their dialogue.

At home

Bill _____I'm_____ hungry.

Angela What _____ to eat?

Bill _____ some chicken.

Angela Let's go _____.

In the car

Bill _____ is the restaurant?

Angela It's that way.

At the restaurant, before eating

Angela What _____ you _____ for the main course?

Bill I'd like _____.

At the restaurant, after eating

Angela Waiter, _____, please?

Challenge

Which foods have you tasted from other countries? Do you like Italian food? Chinese food? Make a list of your favorite kinds of restaurants.

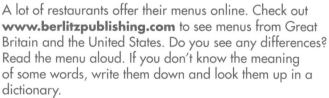

Internet Activity

A lot of restaurants offer their menus online. Check out **www.berlitzpublishing.com** to see menus from Great Britain and the United States. Do you see any differences? Read the menu aloud. If you don't know the meaning of some words, write them down and look them up in a dictionary.

Unit 6 **Weather and Temperature**

In this unit, you will learn:
- to talk about temperature, weather and seasons.
- how to describe things.
- the simple past tense of regular verbs.

LESSON 1

What's the weather like?

Dialogue

Padma lives in New York and Fred lives in Glasgow, Scotland. Listen to their phone conversation about the weather.

Padma Hello, Fred. What's the weather like in Glasgow?

Fred It's cold. It's sunny but it's five degrees Celsius.

Padma Really? It's not very nice here either.

Fred What's the temperature?

Padma Fifty degrees Fahrenheit and it's windy and raining.

Fred Fifty degrees? That's warm!

Activity A

Answer the questions based on the dialogue.

1 What's the temperature in Glasgow?

   It's five degrees Celsius.

2 What's the temperature in New York?

   _____

3 What's the weather like in Scotland?

   _____

4 What's the weather like in New York?

   _____

Activity B

Answer the questions based on the thermometers below.

1 What's the temperature in Fahrenheit in Seoul?

   It's 20 degrees Fahrenheit.

2 What's the temperature in Celsius in Seoul?

   _____

3 What's the temperature in Fahrenheit in Hanoi?

   _____

4 What's the temperature in Celsius in Hanoi?

   _____

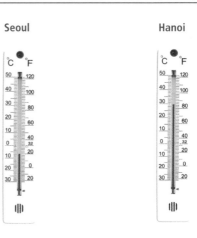

Seoul   Hanoi

SMART TIP

There is more than one way to say *in addition* in English: *also* and *too*. *Too* is always placed at the end of a sentence. *Also* is more formal than *too*.

It's also cold in London.
It's hot in Mexico City, too.

Essential Words

cold
cloudy
hot
humid
It's raining.
It's windy.
rainy
sunny
warm
weather
windy

Activity A

Match each word with the picture it describes.

1 cloudy   a
2 sunny   b
3 windy   c
4 rainy   d

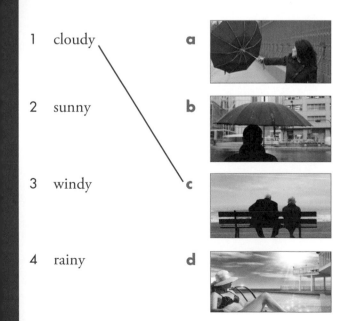

Activity B

Circle the statement that matches each phrase.

1 It's nice out.

   ⓐ It's sixty degrees   **b It's cold.**
   Fahrenheit.

2 It's 2 degrees Celsius outside.

   a It's hot.   **b It's cold.**

3 It's raining and it's windy. This is about:

   a the temperature   **b the weather**

4 It's 50° Fahrenheit outside. This is about:

   a the weather   **b the temperature**

Activity C

What's the weather like right now where you live? Is it sunny and warm? Is it windy and cold? Use the Essential Words and a dictionary to describe your weather.

_____

_____

_____

CULTURE TIPS

- The United States and Great Britain use the Fahrenheit system, not the Celsius system. Canada, like most countries, uses Celsius.

- To change Fahrenheit degrees into Celsius degrees: subtract 32, then multiply by 5, then divide by 9:

  $68°F \longrightarrow 68 - 32 = 36 \times 5 = 180 \div 9 = 20°C$

  To change Fahrenheit degrees into Celsius degrees: subtract 32, then multiply by 5, then divide by 9:

  $20°C \longrightarrow 20 \times 9 = 180 \div 5 = 36 + 32 = 68°F$

- Water freezes at 0°C or 32°F. Water boils at 100°C or 212°F.

LESSON 3

Smart Phrases

Essential Phrases

What's the temperature?
It's … degrees Fahrenheit.
What's the weather like?
It's hot/cold.
It's sunny.
The weather is bad/nice.

the weather forecast
It's raining.
It's snowing.

CULTURE TIP

It's raining cats and dogs (Am.) and
The rain is bucketing down (Brit.)
means it's raining very hard.

Activity A

Put each word or phrase in the correct place.

35°C	65°F	It's warm.
It's raining.	20°C	It's cold.

What's the temperature?	What's the weather like?
_____35°C_____	_____
_____	_____
_____	_____

Activity B

What's the weather like? Match each photo with the correct description of the weather.

1   **a** It's hot.

2   **b** It's sunny.

3   **c** It's rainy.

4   **d** It's cold.

Activity C

Imagine that it's a beautiful spring day. Circle the correct answer.

1 What's the weather like?

   ⓐ It's nice.   **b It's bad.**

2 Is it warm or cold?

   a It's warm.   **b It's cold.**

3 What's the temperature?

   a It's forty degrees Fahrenheit.   **b It's sixty degrees Fahrenheit.**

4 Is it raining or is it sunny?

   a It's sunny.   **b It's raining.**

Smart Grammar

SMART TIP

When two or more adjectives describe the same noun, they are in the following order: opinion (*beautiful, bad*), size (*big, small*), age (*young, old*), color (*red, blue*), origin (*Korean, Canadian*). For example:

a beautiful, big, Korean restaurant

What's it like?

To get a description of something, ask *What's it like?* (sing.) or *What are they like?* (pl.).

Examples

What's the weather like? It's snowing.
What's Vietnam like? It's a beautiful country.
What are your parents like? They're very nice.

Activity A

Match each question with the picture it describes.

1   What does it taste like?

2   What does it look like?

3   What does it feel like?

4   What does it smell like?

5   What does it sound like?

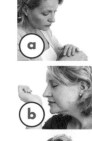

Activity B

Put the phrases in the correct order.

1   ball a red big

   a big red ball

2   sunny a beautiful day

   _____

3   tall young boy a

   _____

4   French car a fast

   _____

Your Turn

Make sentences with adjectives that you know and put the adjectives in their correct place.

What do you do?

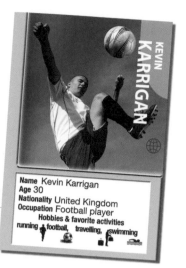

Name Kevin Karrigan
Age 30
Nationality United Kingdom
Occupation Football player
Hobbies & favorite activities
running football, travelling, swimming

Here is an interview with Kevin Karrigan, a famous soccer player. What does Kevin like to do? What does he like to wear during each season?

Interview

Reporter What do you usually do in the summer?

Kevin In summer I play soccer, I swim and I run.

Reporter Do you travel in the summer?

Kevin Yes, I often travel in the summer. I like travelling. It's fun. In winter I stay in the U.S. and in summer I travel to Spain.

Reporter In summer you don't need many clothes, only shorts, a t-shirt and sandals but in winter you need to wear more.

Kevin That's right. It's cold in winter in New York and I wear a hat, a scarf, a coat and gloves.

Reporter Look at this photo. You are with your family. What are you doing?

Kevin We're playing in the snow.

Activity A

Complete the word web with the activities Kevin does in the summer.

summer activities

plays soccer

Complete the word web with the clothes Kevin wears in the winter.

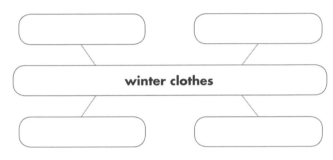

winter clothes

Activity B

Complete the following sentences about Kevin.

1 Kevin swims, runs and __*plays soccer*__ in the summer.

2 In the winter Kevin stays in _____.

3 Kevin travels in the _____.

4 Kevin wears a jacket in the _____.

CULTURE TIP

What the rest of the world calls *football*, Americans call *soccer*. Americans use the word *football* to mean *American football*.

Smart Phrases

Essential Phrases

What do you usually do?
What are you doing?
I play football.
I like travelling.
In the summer, I usually…

It's fun.
It's boring.
That's right.
You need to…

Activity A

What do you think? Use *it's fun* or *it's boring* to say if you find the activities in the pictures boring or not.

1

_____

2

_____

3

_____

4

_____

Activity B

What do you say when you want to…

1   …ask someone what he or she is doing?

   What are you doing?
   _____

2   …ask someone what he or she usually does in the summer?

   _____

3   …tell what you usually do in the winter?

   _____

4   …tell someone he or she is right?

   _____

SMART TIP

Be careful with gerunds. They look like verbs, but they are nouns. Gerunds describe activities.

I am reading right now. (*am reading* = verb)

Reading is fun. (*Reading* = noun)

John is travelling in India. (*is travelling* = verb)

I like travelling. (*travelling* = noun)

Your Turn

Write some activities that you think are fun and some activities that you think are boring.

fun activites   boring activities

_____   _____

_____   _____

_____   _____

Words to Know

Essential Words

Clothes

coat
gloves
hat
jacket
sandals
scarf
shoes
shorts

The Seasons

winter
spring
summer
fall (Am.)/autumn (Brit.)

Activities

to run
to swim
to travel
to wait
to walk
to wear

to need

Activity A

Write the word that corresponds to each picture.

1

<u>shoes</u>

2
_____

3 _____

4 _____

Activity B

Match the words below to the seasons illustrated in the images.

winter	spring	summer	fall

1 <u>fall</u>

2 _____

3 _____

4 _____

Activity C

What clothes do people wear in different seasons? Use the Essential Words and add other words that you know. People wear some clothes, like *hat*, in more than one season.

1 winter   <u>hat</u>

2 spring   _____

3 summer   <u>hat</u>

4 fall   _____

LESSON 8

Smart Grammar

The simple past tense

Regular verbs in the simple past tense end in *–ed*.

to play
I	played
you (sing.)	played
he/she/it	played
we	played
you (pl.)	played
they	played

The simple past tense describes an action that happened in the past (before now). The following time phrases are often used with the simple past:

yesterday
two days/nights ago
last night
last week
last year
last Monday
in 2006

Activity A

Put the following sentences in the simple past.

1   Now Mary works in London, but last year she
    _____worked_____ in Paris.

2   This year we play football, but last year we
    _____ baseball.

3   Now I like coffee, but before I _____
    tea.

4   It looks bad now, but it _____ really
    good when it was new.

Negatives and questions in the simple past tense

Negative sentences are formed with the helping verb *did* (the simple past tense of *do/does*) followed by *not (didn't)* and the base form of a main verb.

I didn't go to school yesterday.
She didn't travel to Asia last year.
We didn't play soccer last week.

Questions are formed with the helping verb *did* followed by the base form of a main verb.

Did you see him last night?	Yes, I did.
Did he work last weekend?	No, he didn't.
Did they go shopping?	No, they didn't.
Did she buy a new hat?	Yes, she did.

Activity B

Ask the correct questions for the following answers.

1   *Did they walk to school?* _____

    Yes, they walked to school.

2   _____

    No, they didn't finish their homework.

3   _____

    Yes, they needed some money.

4   _____

    No, she didn't call.

Activity C

Answer the following questions.

1   Did you finish the cake? No, *I didn't finish the cake.*

2   Did she call John? Yes, _____

3   Did they speak English? No, _____

4   Did they wait for you? Yes, _____

5   Did he need to leave? No, _____

6   Did they walk here? Yes, _____

Activity A

What's the weather like? Look at the pictures and say what the weather is like.

1 _It's raining._____

2 _____

3 _____

4 _____

Activity B

Find the words related to weather and seasons in the word search.

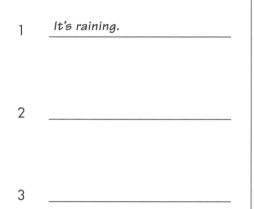

A	P	E	V	Z	L	Z	S	C	S	H	K	W	S	J
X	U	L	A	C	H	A	Q	U	E	T	A	W	U	V
Q	P	T	C	X	Q	Z	M	K	D	Y	D	P	M	C
F	D	S	U	A	P	R	A	I	N	V	E	R	M	E
X	D	W	B	M	N	A	B	R	Z	E	K	P	E	S
Q	Á	L	I	L	N	N	O	L	E	A	D	O	R	T
F	Q	R	A	T	E	M	P	E	R	A	T	U	R	E
P	Z	E	Z	Q	T	Y	M	Q	A	W	P	E	H	R
Y	E	T	T	V	D	E	E	I	D	Y	D	L	L	F
A	I	N	Z	N	A	R	R	G	Q	J	N	J	K	W
B	K	I	I	Z	R	H	R	S	P	R	I	N	G	D
S	Q	W	O	N	S	S	N	U	S	J	R	F	U	U
I	T	Y	T	A	E	Á	R	D	B	X	L	Q	X	S

Activity C

Ask the question that matches the answer.

1 What _does it feel like_____ ? It feels cold.

2 What _____ ? It tastes good.

3 What _____? It smells bad.

4 What _____? It looks nice.

Activity D

What is Petra thinking? Petra invited some friends to have dinner at her home this evening. She is thinking about everything she did and everything she still needs to do. Complete her thoughts.

Did I invite Jorge and Juana?
Yes, I _____ them.

Did I call Leslie?
No, I _____. I need to call her now.

_____ finish cooking the food?
Yes, everything is ready!

Challenge

Look outside. Can you describe the weather? Can you say what activities you'd like to do today?

Example: It's raining, so I'd like to read a book.

Internet Activity

What's the weather like in Great Britain, Canada or Australia? Go to **www.berlitzpublishing.com** for a list of weather forecast sites in English. Then can you find what the weather is like in London, Toronto and Brisbane.

In this unit you will learn:
• vocabulary related to shopping and means of payment.
• to ask for clothing and different sizes in stores.
• to make comparisons.
• the verbs *to try on* and *to put on*.
• to use *much* and *many, how much* and *how many.*

LESSON
1
At the department store

Dialogue

Ann is in a department store. She is looking for a dress. Listen to her conversation with the salesperson.

Salesperson   Hello. Can I help you?

Ann   I'm looking for a summer dress.

Salesperson   Here are some summer dresses. What size are you looking for?

Ann   Medium, please.

Salesperson   And which color would you like?

Ann   I'd like a blue dress.

Salesperson   This dress is very pretty. Would you like to try it on?

Ann   Yes, please.

Activity A
Circle the correct picture.

1   What article of clothing is Ann looking for?

     a   b   c

2   What size does Ann want?

     a   small   b   medium   c   large

3   What color does Ann try on?

     a   b   c

Activity B
Write the salesperson's questions that match Ann's answers.

1   *Can I help you?*

I'm looking for a summer dress.

2   _____

Medium, please.

3   _____

I'd like a blue dress.

4   _____

Yes, please.

2 Smart Phrases

Essential Phrases

Can I help you?

I'm looking for…

I want to buy…

What size are you looking for?

I need a size 10.

I need a medium./I'm a medium.

Do you want to try it on?

I'll try it on.

The shirt is too big/small/tight/loose for me.

Anything else?

Activity A

Choose the correct answer.

1   Hello. Can I help you?

(a) I'm looking for a dress.

b The dress is too small.

2   What size do you need?

a I need a large, please.

b I'd like to buy a coat.

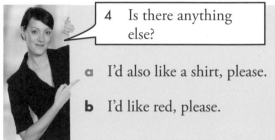

3   Would you like to try it on?

a Yes, please.

b It's too big.

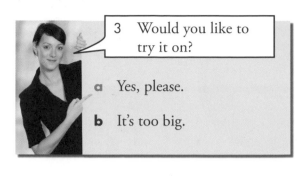

4   Is there anything else?

a I'd also like a shirt, please.

b I'd like red, please.

Activity B

Answer the questions using the phrases you just learned.

1   Can I help you?

I'm looking for a shirt.

Say that you are looking for a shirt..

2   What size?

_____

Say that you need a medium.

3   Anything else?

_____

Say that you want to buy a coat.

4   What color coat would you like?

_____

Say that you'd like a red coat.

SMART TIP

We learned that *too* means *also*. When it is placed before an adjective, it has a negative meaning: *It's too big* = It's very big and that's a problem.

Words to Know

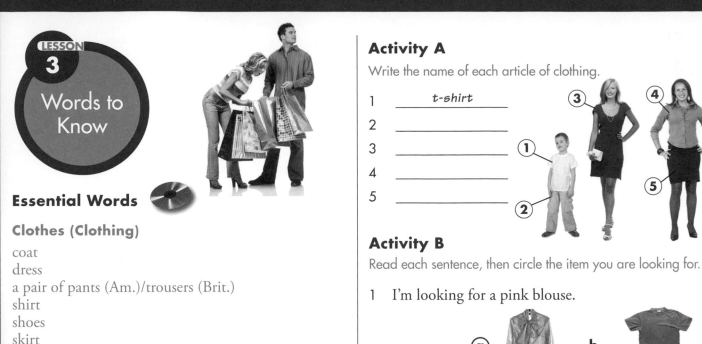

Essential Words

Clothes (Clothing)

coat
dress
a pair of pants (Am.)/trousers (Brit.)
shirt
shoes
skirt
socks
sweater (Am.)/jumper (Brit.)
t-shirt
tie

Sizes

small
medium
large
extra large

Colors (Am.)/Colours (Brit.)

black   purple

blue   red

green   white

pink   yellow

Activity A

Write the name of each article of clothing.

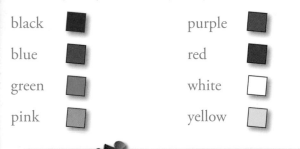

1 _____t-shirt_____
2 _____
3 _____
4 _____
5 _____

Activity B

Read each sentence, then circle the item you are looking for.

1 I'm looking for a pink blouse.

(a)   b

2 I'm looking for a red dress.

a   b

3 I'm looking for a large t-shirt.

a   b

4 I'm looking for a black coat.

a   b

Smart Grammar

Phrasal verbs

Phrasal verbs are sometimes called two-word verbs because they have two parts, a verb and a preposition. The verb plus the preposition has a different meaning than when the verb is alone.

to put means to place:
  I put my book on my desk.

to put on means to get dressed:
  I always put on my socks before I put on my shoes.

to try means to attempt to do something:
  I tried to ski, but it was too difficult.

to try on means to put on clothing to see if it fits:
  I tried on a dress, but it was too big.

to take off means to get undressed:
  I took off my shoes when I got home.

to pick out means to choose which clothing to wear:
  Nancy picked out a green blouse to wear with her black pants.

SMART TIP

In English, *much* comes before uncountable nouns and *many* comes before countable nouns. Both *much* and *many* mean *a lot of* or *lots of*. *A lot of/lots of* is used in positive statements: *Juanita has a lot of shoes.*

A lot of/lots of, much and *many* are all used in negative statements and questions: *Gita doesn't have a lot of/much food in the house, so she needs to go shopping. Do you have a lot of/many ties?*

Use *how much?* to ask about prices: *How much does that dress cost?*

Activity A

Complete the questions using the correct preposition.

1 Can I try _____on_____ this dress please?
2 Did you put _____ the red tie?
3 Did she pick _____ the bag?
4 Can you help me take _____ these boots, please?

Activity B

Complete the questions with *much* for uncountable nouns or *many* for countable nouns.

1 How _____many_____ pairs of shoes do you have?
2 How _____ water do you drink every day?
3 How _____ children do you have?
4 How _____ time do you have?
5 How _____ dresses do you have?

Activity C

Answer the questions by saying that you only have a small quantity: *Do you have any milk? Yes, but I don't have much.; Do you have any potatoes? Yes, but I don't have many.*

1 Do you have any water?
  Yes, but ___I don't have much_____.

2 Do you have any cheese?
  Yes, but _____.

3 Do you have any bananas?
  Yes, but _____.

4 Do you have any juice?
  Yes, but _____.

5 Do you have any vegetables?
  Yes, but _____.

6 Do you have any oranges?
  Yes, but _____.

LESSON 5

How will you pay?

How do you want to pay?

Look at the advertisement for the store UrbanWear.

URBANWEAR

Visit UrbanWear
for the summer sales!
Prices reduced by 50%
on all the Creativ' summer fashions.
Yes, fifty per cent! Top designs at the
lowest prices.
Get 40% off jackets designed
by McCarthy.
Top fashions for less!

CHICWEAR

Visit ChicWear for the summer sales!
Get 20% off
all the Creativ' summer fashions.
Top fashion for less money!
Get 30% off jackets designed
by McCarthy.
Top designs at the lowest prices.

Is tax included?

Yes, all the prices include tax. We don't take credit cards, I'm afraid.

Is tax included?

No, tax is not included. We take credit cards, of course.

Now look at the advertisement for ChicWear. Note the differences between this advertisement and the previous one.

:::
summer sales   jackets designed by…
prices   top fashions
tax   less expensive
reduced   cheap
lowest prices   money
get 30% off
:::

Activity A

Circle the correct answer. Use the UrbanWear ad to help you.

1 What is the sale on Creativ' summer fashions?

   a 40% off   **b 50% off**

2 What is the sale on UrbanWear jackets?

   a 40% off   **b 50% off**

3 When is the sale?

   a in the spring   **b in the summer**

Activity B

Compare the two ads and circle the correct answer.

1 Who has the best sale?

   ⓐ UrbanWear   **b ChicWear**

2 Is the sale on McCarthy jackets better or worse at UrbanWear?

   a better   **b worse**

3 Is tax included in the prices at ChicWear?

   a yes   **b no**

4 Does ChicWear accept credit cards?

   a yes   **b no**

SMART TIP

In the United States, one dollar ($1) is divided into 100 cents. There are 100 cents in a dollar.

In Great Britain, one pound (£1) is divided into 100 pence. There are 100 pence in a pound.

Smart Phrases

Essential Phrases

Do you accept credit cards/checks (Am.)/cheques (Brit.)?

Yes, we accept…

How much is the skirt?

How much are the pants (Am.)/trousers (Brit.)?

It's cheap/They're cheap!

That's (too) expensive!/That's not expensive!

I'll pay by credit card.

Here's your change/receipt.

I want to buy it.

I want to buy them.

I'm just looking.

Activity A

What do you say when you want to…

1 …ask if the store accepts credit cards?

   Do you take credit cards?

2 …ask how much a skirt is?

   _____

3 …ask if the store accepts checks?

   _____

4 …say that you are going to pay with a credit card?

   _____

5 …ask the price of a pair of pants?

   _____

6 …say that you want to buy a skirt?

   _____

Activity B

Look at each picture and choose the best expression.

| expensive | cheap |

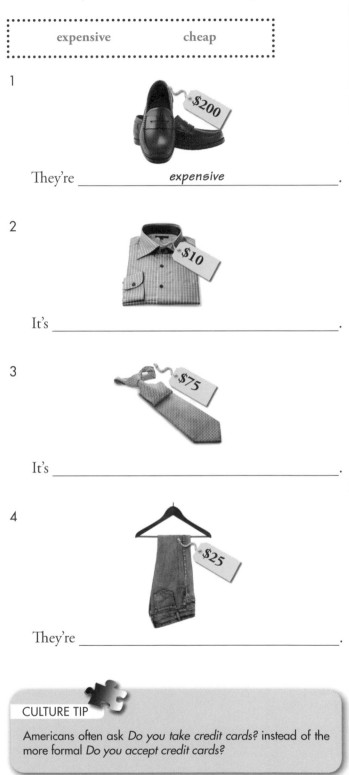

1

They're _____ *expensive* _____.

2

It's _____.

3

It's _____.

4

They're _____.

CULTURE TIP

Americans often ask *Do you take credit cards?* instead of the more formal *Do you accept credit cards?*

LESSON 7

Words to Know

Essential Words

cash
change
coin
credit card
money
receipt
tax (Am.)/VAT (Brit.)
wallet

Activity A

Use the pictures to complete the sentences.

1   Do you take _____?

2   Can I pay with a _____?

3   Here's your _____.

Activity B

Fill in the blanks with *much* or *many* in the conversation between Pooja and James.

Pooja   I want to buy those dresses but I don't have
_____*much*_____ money. How about you?

James   I don't have _____ money but I've
got five credit cards.

Pooja   Really? I haven't got _____ credit
cards but I've got some cash and a check book.

James   How _____ cash do you have?

Pooja   I have $78 in cash.

James   Good. I think we have enough to pay for
some dresses. How _____ dresses
do you want?

Your Turn

Answer the questions about money in your country.

1   What kind of money is used in your country?
Pesos, yuan, won, rupees?

_____

2   Do people in your country usually pay with cash
or credit cards?

_____

3   Do people in your country pay sales tax?

_____

SMART TIP

Note that in English you pay *with* a credit card, *by* check
and *in* cash.

LESSON 8

Smart Grammar

More than, less than

More… than and *less… than* compare two things.

more than >
less than <

Examples

I have *more money* than Julie.
Julie has *less money* than me.
The coat coasts *more (money)* than the tie.
The tie costs *less (money)* than the coat.

Activity A

Compare the articles of clothing and say which one costs more and which one costs less. Fill in the blanks with *more than* or *less than*.

1   The dress costs ___more than___ the shirt.

2   The pants cost _____ the jacket.

3   The shirt costs _____ the jacket.

4   The jacket costs _____ the pants.

$100

$45

$20

$60

Indefinite Pronouns

In Unit 4, we saw that the indefinite article *some* becomes *any* in a question or a negative statement. Here are pronouns that follow the same model:

someone (somebody)
anyone (anybody)
something/anything

Examples

I know someone from Canada.
Do you know anyone from New Zealand?
No, I don't know anyone from there.

When *else* is added to these forms, it means *other: someone else, anything else.*

Do you want just the coat or would you like to try on anything else? Maybe a blouse?
Is that your cousin Marco? No, it's not him. It's someone else.

Activity B

Circle the correct indefinite pronoun for each sentence.

1   Does **anyone**/**anything** want to eat?

2   **Anybody/Someone** here speaks Chinese.

3   Do you want **anything/someone** to eat?

4   Did you buy **anything/somebody** else?

> **SMART TIP**
>
> To say that two things are identical (equal), you can say *the same as…*
>
> The same as =
>
> *The shirt costs the same as the pants.*

Unit 7 Review

Activity A

Complete the conversation between Simon and the salesperson with *much* or *many*.

Simon Hello, I'd like to look at that blue shirt. How _____*much*_____ is it, please? And do you have the shirt in any other color?

Salesperson It's $25. Yes, we have several colors.

Simon How _____ colors do you have?

Salesperson There are four colors. Red, yellow, blue and green.

Simon I'd like two green shirts, three blue shirts and one red shirt, please!

Salesperson Sorry, how _____ blue shirts do you want?

Simon I want three, please.

Salesperson That's a lot of shirts. Are they for you?

Simon No, they're for my cousins. How _____ is that altogether, please?

Salesperson That's $150, please. How would you like to pay?

Simon With a credit card.

Activity B

Say out loud which articles are more expensive and less expensive. Then, write two sentences using *more than* and *less than*.

Activity C

Using the photos, complete the crossword puzzle with the correct English word.

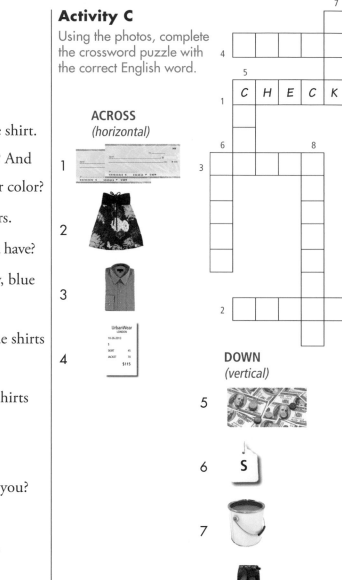

ACROSS *(horizontal)*

1

2

3

4

DOWN *(vertical)*

5

6 S

7

8

Internet Activity

Go to **www.berlitzpublishing.com** for a selection of online clothing stores. Look through each website to see what they offer. Take advantage of the opportunity to discover new words related to clothing.

1 $ 21 $ 30

2 $ 40 $ 60

3 $ 160 $ 90

4 $ 15 $ 20

Unit 8 Travel and Vacation

In this unit you will learn:
- **to ask for directions.**
- **to find different geographical locations.**
- **to talk about travel plans.**
- **irregular verbs in the simple past tense.**
- **the simple future tense with** *be going to* **and** *will*.

LESSON 1 — Where's the station?

Dialogue

Muhammad and Amina are visiting New York for the first time. They are trying to find their way to the Tourism Information Center in Times Square. Listen to them discussing which way to go.

Muhammad Look, we're here in Central Park. How do we get to the Tourist Information Center?

Amina Look at the map. Times Square is in Midtown West near Broadway. We can take the bus or the subway.

Muhammad But we're not very far, you know. Let's walk there.

Amina But the subway is just over there in front of the post office.

Muhammad No, let's walk. Then we can see the streets and buildings in New York. I want to see the buildings and the shops.

Amina OK. Let's go!

> **SMART TIP**
>
> *Let's …* is frequently used to suggest to another person that you want the two of you to do something together. The other person is free to accept or to refuse your suggestion! For example:
>
> *Let's walk to Times Square. Let's get directions.*

Activity A

Match each verb to its picture.

> take   walk   fly

1 _____

2 _____

3 _____

Activity B

Answer the questions.

1 Where are Muhammad and Amina?
   They're in Central Park in New York.

2 Where do they want to go? _____

3 How can they get there? _____

4 Does Amina prefer to walk? _____

Words to Know

Essential Words 🔘

Places

bus stop
church
library
post office
school
subway (Am.)/underground
   station (Brit.)
supermarket
train station
Tourism Information Center (Am.)/
   Centre (Brit.)

Location

behind
far
in front of
near
next to
on/to the left
on/to the right
opposite (across from)
block
corner

SMART TIPS

• To ask for directions, use the verb *to get to: Excuse me, how do I get to the station?*

• To give directions, use the imperative, which is the base form of the verb. The understood subject *you* isn't used.

   Turn left/right. Go straight (Am.)/straight on (Brit.). Cross the street. Go past the church.

Activity A

Label each picture with the correct English word.

library
where you borrow books

where you get
the subway

where you learn

where you pray

where you get the train

where you wait for the bus

where you mail letters

where you buy food

Activity B

Circle the location of each building.

1   The subway station is _____ of the library.

     a to the left   **ⓑ to the right**

2   The school is _____ the train station.

     a far from   **b near**

3   The post office is _____ the supermarket.

     a across from   **b next to**

4   The bus stop is _____ the church.

     a across from   **b next to**

Essential Phrases

Where is…?
How do I get to…?
To get to…, take bus number…
I want to take the train/bus.
I want to take the subway (Am.)/underground (Brit.).
The train station is near the school.

Let's get a map.
Excuse me.
Thanks a lot.
You're welcome.

Activity A

Write that you want to take the means of transportation shown in each picture. Then, ask where you can find the stop or station.

1    *I want to take the bus.*

   Where is the bus stop?

2

3

Activity B

What do you say when you want to…

1 …ask where the train station is?

   Where is the train station?

2 …ask how to get to the subway station?

3 …tell someone the train station is near the school?

4 …suggest that you and your friend buy a map?

Activity C

A tourist asks you for help getting from New York to Boston. She needs to take the bus to the train station and then take the train. Tell her how to get to the bus stop, to take bus number 9 and to get off the bus at Penn Station. Tell her how to get to Boston.

Tourist How do I get to Boston, please?

You Well, first *go to the bus stop across*

   the street.

Your Turn

You want to go to the bus stop. Ask where it is and how to get there.

Smart Grammar

The simple past tense of irregular verbs

In Unit 6 we saw that forming regular simple past tense verbs is quite easy (add the ending –ed for all subjects). Irregular verbs except for *to be* also have one form for all subjects, but they do not end in –ed.

For example: *to have* becomes *had* in the simple past tense.

I have → *I had*
you (sing.) have → *you had*
he/she/it has → *he/she/it had*
we have → *we had*
you (pl.) have → *you had*
they have → *they had*

We had dinner at 7:30 PM last night.

to be
I am → *I was*
you (sing.) are → *you were*
he/she/it is → *he/she/it was*
we are → *we were*
you (pl.) are → *you were*
they are → *they were*

I was at home yesterday, but you were at work.

Other examples:

buy → bought	know → knew
come → came	leave → left
do → did	read → read
eat → ate	say → said
find → found	see → saw
fly → flew	sleep → slept
go → went	take → took
get → got	tell → told
hear → heard	write → wrote

See page XXX for a list of other irregular past tense verbs.

The simple past tense of *read* looks like the base form of the verb, but it's pronounced like the color red.

Activity A

Complete the letter by filling in the blanks with simple past tense verbs. Some verbs are regular and some are irregular.

Dear Catalina,

Here I am in Canada. It _____was_____ (be) a long journey but the weather is very nice. Yesterday I _____ (take) the plane at eight thirty and I _____ (arrive) here at ten o'clock in the morning. I _____ (go) to the hotel and _____ (go) to bed! I _____ (sleep) for one hour and then _____ (go) downtown. I _____ (see) a lot of interesting buildings and stores there. I _____ (buy) some postcards and _____ (eat) a hamburger and then I _____ (come) back to the hotel.

Love,
Pierre

Activity B

Change the present tense sentences to the past tense.

1   I eat breakfast at 8:00 AM.
    I ate breakfast at 8:00 AM.

2   Monica takes the bus.
    _____

3   Jung Yun is in Korea.
    _____

4   We have a nice hotel.
    _____

Traveling

Arrivals and Departures

Florian wrote an e-mail to Petra about his trip to Dublin, Ireland.

Date :   Tuesday April 13
From :   Florian
To :   Petra
Subject :   Dublin

Hi Petra!
Last month I went on vacation. I went to to Dublin! I got the plane tickets, booked the hotel and packed my suitcase. I took flight number 124 and flew from Berlin to Dublin. The plane left Berlin at 11:30 AM and arrived in Dublin at 12:50 PM. I took the bus from the airport to the hotel.
Florian

SMART TIP

Note the use of prepositions in the above e-mail: *at 11:30 AM, to Dublin, to the hotel, in Dublin, from the airport.*

To describes movement toward a place, *in* describes the location inside a place or thing and *at* is used to express the time.

At can also be used to describe a place: *at the train station, at my brother's office, at home, at the window.*

Activity A

Circle the correct answer.

1 Where did Florian go on vacation?
   ⓐ Dublin   **b Berlin**
2 When did he leave Berlin?
   a last week   **b last month**
3 When did the airplane leave Berlin?
   a 11:30 AM   **b 12:50 PM**
4 How did he get to the hotel from the airport?
   a by bus   **b by car**

Activity B

Florian returned to Berlin and e-mailed Petra about his flight home. Look at the information below and complete Florian's e-mail.

🌐 ReganAir			**RA649**
Departs	**Time**	**Arrives**	**Time**
Dublin International Airport	12:00 PM	Berlin International Airport	1:00 PM

Date :   Wednesday April 21
From :   Florian
To :   Petra
Subject :   flight home

Hi Petra,
Here is the information for my flight home.
It left Dublin at_____.
I arrived in Berlin at_____.
Florian

LESSON 6

Words to Know

Essential Words

airport
flight
luggage
passport
plane
suitcase
ticket
trip
vacation (Am.)/holidays (Brit.)

hotel
reservation/booking
stop/layover

SMART TIPS

- In American English a *holiday* is a day when people don't have to go to work: *I like to travel during holidays.* When people travel for pleasure, they *go on a vacation* (Am.)/*go on holiday* (Brit.): *Bill and Carl went to San Francisco on vacation (Am.)/holiday (Brit.) last summer.*

- Detailed travel plans including transportation (airplane, train, bus) dates and times, hotel reservations and planned number of days in each location is called an *itinerary.*

Activity A

Draw a line to match each word to its picture.

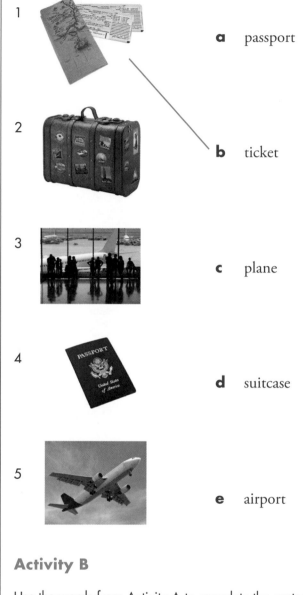

1

a passport

2

b ticket

3

c plane

4

d suitcase

5

e airport

Activity B

Use the words from Activity A to complete the sentences.

1 You put your clothes in a ____*suitcase*____ when you travel.

2 You can also call an *airplane* a _____.

3 You go to the _____ to get on a plane.

4 You need a _____ to travel internationally.

5 You buy a _____ to get on a plane or train.

Essential Phrases

How much does the flight cost?
A round trip (Am.)/return (Brit.) ticket costs $500.
What (or Which) is the departure gate?
What (or Which) is the arrival gate?
When is the next flight to Sydney?

Activity A

What do you say when you want to…

1   …tell your friend that your flight arrived at 12:30 PM?

My flight arrived at 12:30 PM.

2   …ask where the departure gate is?

_____

3   …ask how much the ticket costs?

_____

4   …tell your friend that you want to go to a nice hotel?

_____

CULTURE TIP

A ticket to go and return is called a
round trip ticket in the United States and
a *return ticket* in Great Britain. A ticket
that only goes and does not return is
called a *one-way ticket* in the United States and a *single
ticket* in Great Britain.

PRONUNCIATION TIP

The *gh* in English is usually not pronounced if it follows an *i:*
night [naïtt], *flight* [flaïtt]. Sometimes it sounds like an *f: laugh*
[laff], *enough* [inaff].

Activity B

Armanda is at the ticket counter asking about the next
available flight to Sydney. Circle the correct answers to
her questions.

1   When is the next flight to Sydney?

   a The flight leaves at 8 o'clock.

   b The flight arrives at 8 o'clock.

2   How much does the ticket cost?

   a The plane leaves soon.

   b It costs $800 for a round-trip ticket.

3   Where is the arrival gate?

   a Gate 5.   **b I'm sorry, you can't go.**

Activity C

Look at the departure screen below and answer
the questions.

DEPARTURES		
Time	Destination	Flight
4:15 PM	Dallas	EZY5258
4:35 PM	Los Angeles	EZY5259
5:00 PM	New York	MZY448058
5:00 PM	Miami	VZX7250
5:20 PM	Memphis	VZX7251
5:25 PM	Seattle	LNN4432

1   When was the flight to Seattle?
   The flight to Seattle was at 5:25 PM.

2   Which flight departed at 4:35 PM?

   _____

3   Where did flight VZX7250 arrive?

   _____

4   When was the flight to Memphis?

   _____

Your Turn

Imagine you work for British Airways. Announce the
next flight for New York: Flight 1699, departing at
10:23 AM, arriving at 1:30 PM.

Smart Grammar

The simple future tense

The simple future tense describes an action that will happen in the future (after now). Both the modal *will* and be *going to* + the base form of the main verb are forms of the simple future tense.

Will is often contracted: *I'll see you soon. We'll have a nice time in Rome.*

Examples

Giang and I <u>are going to</u>/<u>will</u> travel to Scotland tomorrow morning.
<u>She's going to</u>/<u>She'll</u> take the train at 9:00 AM.
<u>We're going to</u>/<u>We'll</u> arrive next Thursday.

SMART TIP

The following time phrases are often used with the simple future:

in two days/2025/three minutes
next week/month/year/Tuesday
soon
tomorrow
tomorrow morning/afternoon/evening/night

Activity A

What do you say when you want to…

1   …tell your parents that your flight will arrive at Gate 10?   *My flight will arrive at Gate 10.*

2   ….ask when your flight is going to depart?
_____

3   …ask your friends where they are going on their vacation? _____

4   …tell your sister that you will meet her at the train station? _____

SMART TIPS

- Use the modal *will* when you are 100% sure about a future action. Use the modals *may* and *might* when you are about 50% sure: *I definitely will go to Spain next summer, but I'm not sure which city to visit. I may/might go to Barcelona or I may/might go to Granada. I'll decide on Saturday.*

- In British English the modal *shall* is also used when you are 100% sure about a future action: *I shall have you over to my house for tea very soon.*

Activity B

Write about what you may/might do next weekend.

Next weekend I might _____

SMART TIP

Sometimes the simple present tense and the present progressive tense also describe the future. The simple present describes schedules: *My plane leaves at 10:25 PM.* The present progressive describes future plans: *I'm visiting Paris next year.*

Activity C

Circle the correct answer.

1   Which sentence describes the future?

   a Brigitte's bus leaves at 8:30 every morning.
   ⓑ Brigitte's bus leaves at 8:30 tomorrow morning.

2   Which sentence describes the present?

   a I'm having dinner at the restaurant soon.
   b I'm having dinner at the restaurant right now.

3   Which sentence describes the present?

   a We're traveling to Vietnam next spring.
   b We're traveling in Vietnam, and it's very hot today.

4   Which sentence describes the future?

   a I need to go to the airport in a few minutes because my flight leaves in two hours.
   b I always go to the airport two hours before my flight leaves.

Activity A

Complete the sentences with simple past tense verbs. Some verbs are regular and some are irregular.

1 Yesterday, we ____*went*____ (go) shopping.

2 We _____ (walk) to our favorite store.

3 We _____ (look) at the clothes on sale.

4 He _____ (buy) three shirts on sale.

5 They _____ (get) a pair of shoes.

6 You _____ (be) very happy!

Activity B

The words in each sentence below have been mixed up. Try to put them in the correct order to complete Tony's itinerary. The first and last sentences are already correct.

My trip to London

Tomorrow I'm going to London, England.

My leaves at flight the 8 o'clock morning in.

I be o'clock at airport the at must six.

It's early very!

I luggage have ticket my and passport my and my.

London I o'clock arrive in at 10 find and then I must go hotel the bus to to the.

Trafalgar Square The is near hotel.

behind It's church a.

National Gallery Tomorrow I to want visit the to and then the Tate Museum go.

I English money need some.

Where it put did I?

Ah, I have it.

Activity C

Circle the correct answer.

1 Tomorrow I _____ go to the library.
   ⓐ will   **b don't**

2 Last weekend we _____ to a museum.
   a went   **b are going**

3 Next Tuesday Sharon and Pete _____ to Brazil.
   a are going to fly   **b flew**

4 Two weeks ago my brother and sister _____ lunch together.
   a are eating   **b ate**

Challenge

Complete the table of irregular verbs below.

bring	brought
see	
	wore
read	
	paid
put	
	flew
speak	
	wrote
swim	
	cost

Internet Activity

Go to **www.berlitzpublishing.com** to search for the cheapest flight to New York on the date of your choice. You'll need to answer some questions: Where are you leaving from? What is your departure date? What is your return date? What time is the flight? How much is the flight?

Unit 9 Professions

In this unit you will learn:
- **to describe and compare professions.**
- **to use questions and negative statements in the simple future tense with *will*.**
- **to fill out a job application.**
- **to talk about what you do for a living**

LESSON 1

Job interview

Dialogue

Rose is interviewing for a job at the newspaper the *Daily News*. Listen to her answer questions about her previous job.

Employer	Where have you worked?
Rose	I worked for a magazine, *The Weekly World*.
Employer	Did you write articles for the magazine?
Rose	Yes, I wrote several articles.
Employer	What subjects did you write about?
Rose	I wrote about popular culture. Here are some of the articles.
Employer	These articles are very good! You have the job.
Rose	Thank you very much! When can I start?
Employer	Next Monday. I'll see you on Monday at 9 o'clock.

SMART TIPS
- To make negative statements in the future, *will* is followed by *not* (*I will not work on Sunday.*). *Will not* is usually shortened to *won't* (*I won't go on a job interview tomorrow.*).
- To ask questions with *will*, place it before the subject and the base form of the main verb: *Will you look for a new job? Yes, I will/No, I won't. Will Rose start her new job on Monday? Yes, she will/No, she won't.*

Activity A

Circle the correct answer.

1 Where did Rose work?
   a for a newspaper   **(b)** for a magazine
2 What did Rose do at her previous job?
   a She wrote articles.   **b** She made TV programs.
3 What does Rose show to the interviewer?
   a photos   **b** articles
4 Does Rose get the job?
   a yes   **b** no

Activity B

Choose a word from the box to complete each sentence.

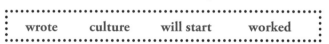

wrote	culture	will start	worked

1 Rose _____worked_____ for a magazine.
2 Rose _____ articles for a magazine.
3 She wrote articles about _____.
4 Rose_____ on Monday at 9 o'clock.

Activity C

Answer the questions.

1 Will Rebecca work for a magazine? Yes, she ___*will*___.
2 Will Leon get the job? No, he _____.
3 Will Jim and Roger arrive on time? Yes, _____.
4 Will Sally meet her boss for lunch? No, she _____.

LESSON 2

Words to Know

Essential Words

classroom
job
journalist
magazine
newspaper
office
student
teacher

article
employer

> **SMART TIPS**
>
> - The names of professions have changed in English. In the past people said *salesman* and *saleswoman*, but now people say *salesperson*.
>
>   fireman → *firefighter*
>   mailman → *mail carrier*
>   policemen/policewomen → *police officers*
>
> - To talk about a person's profession or occupation, use the indefinite article: *I'm a doctor. She's a student. He's a cook.* Don't use an article for plurals: *They're journalists. We're salespeople. You're writers.*

Activity A

Which Essential Words are related to school? Which are related to work?

School	Work
classroom	

Activity B

Answer the questions about yourself.

1   Are you a student? If yes, where do you go to school?

_____

_____

2   Are you working? If yes, where do you work?

_____

_____

Activity C

Label each picture with the correct English word and article.

a   *a classroom*
b
c

a
The Daily Press
b
c

Smart Phrases

Essential Phrases

What do you do (for a living)?
I'm a journalist.
I'm a teacher.
What do you want to do later on in life?
I want to be a teacher.
You've got the job.

Activity A

What do you do for a living? Complete the sentences to say what each person does for a living.

1 I'm ____a teacher____   2 I'm _____

What do you want to do later? Look at these pictures and say what these people want to do later on in life.

3 _____   4 _____

Activity B

What do you say when you want to...

1   ...ask someone what his or her profession is?
    What do you do (for a living)?
    _____

2   ...say that you are a journalist?
    _____

3   ...ask someone what she wants to do later on in life?
    _____

4   ...say that you want to be a teacher?
    _____

5   ... say that you are a salesperson?
    _____

Your Turn

Imagine that you are a journalist. You meet a teacher. Ask him what and where he teaches. Ask him how old his students are. Ask him what he likes and doesn't like about his job. Ask him when he decided to be a teacher. Write out your questions and answers.

_____
_____
_____
_____
_____
_____
_____
_____

LESSON 4

Smart Grammar

The present perfect tense with regular past participles

The present perfect tense describes an action that started in the past and is still happening in the present.

For the present perfect tense, use *have/has* and the past participle of the main verb. Regular past participles have the same form as regular simple past tense verbs and end in *–ed*: *Elena and Eduardo have studied English since 2007.* Subject pronouns and *have/has* are often contracted: *I've lived in Mexico City for five years.*

To make negative statements, *have/has* is followed by *not* and is often contracted: *Fabio hasn't worked as a firefighter for five years.*

To ask yes/no questions, place *have/has* before the subject and main verb: *Have you studied English for a long time? Yes, I have/No, I haven't.*

To ask information questions, place *have/has* after the question word: *Where has Sally worked for three years? In a hospital.*

The following phrases are often used with the present perfect:

already
ever
for
since
yet

SMART TIP

For and *since* both talk about the length of time of an action. *Since* tells when the action started. *For* tells the duration of the action (how long it has lasted).

I have studied English since 2008/for two years.

He has lived in New Delhi since January/for six months.

Activity A

Complete the sentences with the present perfect tense of the verb *to work*.

1 She ____*has worked*____ all day.

2 _____ they _____ since Monday?

3 We _____ a lot this year.

4 Where _____ you _____ this week?

5 _____ for a long time and now I'm tired!

Activity B

Use the answers to complete the questions.

1 How long ____*has she lived here*____ ?

She has lived here for six years.

2 Where _____ for 10 months?

They have lived in Arizona.

3 How long _____ ?

I've studied English for many years

4 Have _____?

Yes, I've worked as a police officer for a long time.

Your Turn

Answer the questions about yourself.

1 Where do you live? How long have you lived there?

_____

2 Do you have a job? How long have you worked there?

_____

3 How long have you studied English?

_____

LESSON 5
Job Hunting

A Job Application

Richard is applying for a job as Human Resources Coordinator at Sands Electronics, Inc. Here is his application.

Sands Electronics, Inc.
Application form

Richard Brown	923 383 5890
Name	Phone number

25 Jackson Lane, Newark, NJ 07030
Address

EDUCATION

University	Bergen Business School
Major	Business
From – to	2004 – 2007

EMPLOYMENT

Employer	Job Consulting Inc.
Position	Human Resources Assistant
From – to	October 2008 – present
Manager	Michael Somerfield
Employer	NatWest Bank
Position	Human Resources Assistant
From – to	June 2007 – September 2008
Manager	Jeff Johnson
Last salary:	$35,000
Expected salary:	$40,000

Position applied for:
Human Resources Coordinator

Why are you applying for this position?
To gain more experience in a larger company and to have more responsibility.

SMART TIP

Common word endings for professions are -er/-or and -ist: bank teller, doctor, engineer, lawyer, reporter, writer dentist, florist, journalist, pharmacist

Activity A

Complete the sentences with information from the application.

1 Richard brown is applying for a job as a
   <u>human resources coordinator</u>.

2 He studied at Bergen Business School for
   _____ years.

3 His first job was at _____.

4 From October 2008 to present, he has worked at
   _____.

5 He is applying to Sands Electronics because he
   wants to _____.

SMART TIP

In Lesson 4 we learned that *for* tells the duration of an activity. It can be used with different verb tenses: *I will study for one hour tomorrow. I studied for one hour last night. I have studied for one hour and will stop soon.*

Activity B

Carefully read the following two sentences.

1 He worked at NatWest Bank for two years.

2 He has worked at NatWest Bank for two years.

Why is the simple past used in the first sentence and the present perfect in the second?

SMART TIPS

- In Lesson 4, we learned that the present perfect describes an action that started in the past and is still happening in the present. Sometimes it can describe an action that started and ended in the past (not using *for* or *since*): *Juanita has lived in Mexico, but now she lives in Columbia.*

  Use the simple past tense, not the present perfect, when the time that the action happened is mentioned: *I have worked in a bank. I worked in a bank last year/two months ago/in 2008.*

- The word *ever* is often used in questions and means *at any time: Have you ever been to Venice? Have you ever worked for a big company?*

Words to Know

Essential Words

assistant

boss

employee

job

salary

secretary

business

company

difficult

easy

a lot

Activity A

Circle the correct answer.

1   Which word describes the worker at a job?

(a) employee   b boss   c salary

2   Which word describes the person who gives instructions?

a assistant   b boss   c secretary

3   Which word describes a place of business?

a company   b boss   c employee

4   What do you call the money you earn for your work?

a employee   b salary   c business

Activity B

Complete the crossword puzzle with the Essential Words.

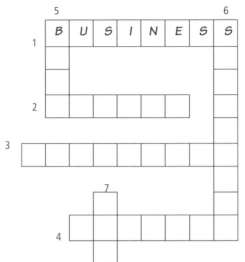

Across

1   A company that earns money.

2   The money you get for your work.

3   The person who helps the boss.

4   Where you work.

Down

5   The person in charge.

6   I'm a businessman. Here is my _____. She helps me in my job.

7   What you do every day.

Your Turn

Imagine that you have your own company. Make a list of people that you will need to work with. How many employees will there be? How many will be assistants and secretaries? What will be the salary of each employee?

LESSON 7

Smart Phrases

Essential Phrases

Why do you want this position?
Because I want to be a journalist.
I like to help.
I like to write.
How long have you worked there?
I have worked there for three months.
It's easier than…
It's harder than…

It pays more.
It pays less.

SMART TIP

For comparisons, add the ending –er to an adjective that has one syllable: *My new job is harder than my old job.* (hard → harder)

When an adjective ends in –e, add –r: *My new boss is nicer than my old one.* (nice → nicer)

When an adjective ends in –y, change it to –i and add –er: *My old job was easier than my new job.* (easy → easier)

When an adjective ends in a vowel + consonant, double the consonant: *My new office is bigger than my old one.* (big → bigger) Don't double the consonant if the adjective ends in –w or –y: (slow → slower)

When an adjective has two or more syllables, place the word *more* before it: *My new job is more interesting than my old job.* (interesting → more interesting)

Some adjectives have irregular comparative forms:
good → better
bad → worse

Activity A

What do you say when you want to…

1 …ask someone why he or she wants to be a journalist?

   Why do you want to be a journalist?

2 …tell someone that you like to help other people?

   _____

3 …ask someone how long he or she has worked in a big company?

   _____

4 …tell someone that you have worked at your company for two years?

   _____

Activity B

Fill in the blanks with the correct form of the comparative.

1 In winter Manila is _____ than Montreal.
   _{hot}

2 This restaurant has _____ food than the
   _{good}
   restaurant we ate at last week.

3 The red dress is _____ than the blue dress.
   _{expensive}

4 A plane is _____ than a train.
   _{fast}

5 Doing housework is _____ than shopping!
   _{boring}

Activity C

What do you think? In your opinion, which is *easier* or *more difficult?* Use a dictionary to look up the words in the box and then answer the questions.

> engineer   lawyer   carpenter   doctor   dentist

1 It's _____ *easier* _____ to be a secretary than a doctor.

2 It's _____ to be an engineer than a teacher.

3 It's _____ to be a lawyer than a journalist.

4 It's _____ to be a carpenter than a dentist.

LESSON 8
Smart Grammar

Irregular past participles

In Lesson 4 we learned that the present perfect of regular verbs is formed with the helping verb *to have* followed by the past participle of the verb (the base form + *-ed*). Like simple past tense verbs, there are many irregular past participles.

Here are some examples:

be → been
do → done
eat → eaten
drink → drunk
get → gotten(Am.)/got (Brit.)
go → gone
have → had
speak → spoken
write → written

See page XXX for a list of other irregular past participles.

Activity A

Complete the table with the missing verb forms.

Activity B

Complete the sentences with the present perfect tense.

1 We ___*have read*___ a lot of newspaper articles this week.
   read

2 Selena _____ Spanish for three years.
   teach

3 Jill and Jack _____ friends since high school.
   be

4 I _____ a lot of good teachers.
   have

5 Pete _____ lunch with his boss every day since he started working for her.
   eat

6 Eleanor _____ her homework.
   do

Base Form	Simple Past	Past Participle
	bought	bought
do		done
	drove	
	ate	eaten
		gone
	got	
leave		left
say	said	
	spoke	
	took	
		written

Unit 9 Review

Activity A

Circle the correct answer.

1 Which sentence describes a completed action?

   a They have lived in New York for many years.
   ⓑ They lived in New York for many years.

2 Which sentence describes an action that is still happening?

   a Carlos has been a lawyer since he graduated from college.
   b Carlos has been a lawyer.

3 Which sentence describes an action that is still happening?

   a We eaten lunch with our boss since last October.
   b We ate lunch with our boss last October.

4 Which sentence describes a completed action?

   a Rosa had a job interview.
   b Rosa has had a lot of job interviews since she left her last job.

Activity B

Complete the questions. Be sure to use the correct verb tense.

1 When *will they work* ?
They will work next Saturday.

2 Where _____?
She worked in Paris.

3 Why _____?
He works because he needs the money.

4 What _____?
He is an engineer.

5 Which _____?
She has the office next to her secretary.

Activity C

Answer the questions using the comparative.

1 Which country is bigger, the United States or New Zealand?

   The United States is bigger than New Zealand.

2 Which river is longer, the Nile or the Mississippi?

_____

3 Which city is colder in winter, Hanoi or Madrid?

_____

4 Which is taller, the Eiffel Tower or Big Ben?

_____

Activity D

Answer the questions about yourself.

1 Have you had many jobs?
2 How many job interviews have you had?
3 Which is easier for you, studying or working?
4 Which is more difficult for you, speaking in English or writing in English?

Challenge

Look at page XXX to find the simple past and past participle forms of these irregular verbs: *to cost, to cut, to hit, to let, to put, to set, to shut.*

What do you notice? What do they have in common?

Internet Activity

Go to **www.berlitzpublishing.com** for a selection of search engines in English to look for a job. How many jobs for assistants can you find? Jobs for secretaries and sales reps (representatives)? What are the salaries for each job?

Unit 10 At Home/Going Out

In this unit you will learn:
- to talk about things to do in a house and in an apartment.
- conditional sentences.
- to use the imperative to give instructions.
- expressions related to going out.
- the past progressive verb tense.

LESSON 1

Help me, please!

An e-mail from Elizabeth

Elizabeth is writing an e-mail to her brother, John. She is asking him to help her clean her apartment.

```
Date:      Tuesday, 10 January
From:      Elizabeth
To:        John
Subject:   Help!

Hi John,
Can you help me to clean my apartment, please? Mom
and Dad are arriving tomorrow and the apartment is
a real mess. I want to pick up my clothes, make my
bed, and tidy up the living room. Then I want to
clean the floor and paint my bedroom. How can you
help me? It would be wonderful if you could help
me pick up my clothes and tidy up the living room.
Then we could clean the floor and paint the walls
together. Can you help me, please?
Much love,
Elizabeth
```

a mess	to clean	don't worry
to pick up	to paint	together
to tidy up	make the bed	

Activity A

Circle the correct answer.

1. What does Elizabeth need help with?
   - **a** her house
   - **(b)** her apartment

2. Who is coming to visit Elizabeth tomorrow?
   - **a** her parents
   - **b** her brother

3. What does Elizabeth ask John?
   - **a** to do the shopping
   - **b** to pick up her clothes

4. What does Elizabeth want John to do with her?
   - **a** organize her papers
   - **b** paint

Activity B

Here is John's response to Elizabeth. Read it carefully and answer the questions.

```
Date:      Tuesday, 10 January
From:      Elisabeth
To:        John
Subject:   Help!

Hi Elizabeth,
Yes, I'll help you. But I don't want to pick up
your clothes. You can pick up your clothes, and
I'll tidy up the living room. Then we can clean
and paint together. Don't worry. I'll help you.
See you soon,
John
```

1. Is John going to help Elizabeth?
   Yes, he will.

2. What does John not want to do?
   _____

3. What does John want to do?
   _____

4. What does John want to do with Elizabeth?
   _____

Words to Know

Essential Words

apartment (Am.)/flat (Brit.)
bathroom
bedroom
dining room
kitchen
living room
room

stairs
garden
floor
window

Activity A

Complete the conversation. Give answers about your house or apartment.

Friend Do you live in a house or in an apartment?

You I live in a(n) _____.

Friend How many rooms are there?

You _____.

Friend How many windows are in each room?

You _____.

Friend Which is your favorite room?

You _____.

Friend Do you have a garden?

You _____.

Activity B

Match each word to its picture.

bathroom	bedroom	living room
kitchen	dining room	

1 _____living room_____   2 _____

3 _____   4 _____

5 _____

CULTURE TIPS

- The floor of a house or a building is called a *floor* or *story* (Am.)/*storey* (Brit.). For parking structures or airports, the word *level* is used.

  The lowest floor is called the *first floor* (Am.)/*ground floor* (Brit.). For example, the *third floor* of a building in the United States is two floors above the ground floor.

- In the United States, ask for the *restroom* or the *bathroom*. In Great Britain, you can ask *Where's the toilet?* or more informally *Where's the loo?* In Canada, it's common to ask for the *washroom*.

Smart Phrases

Essential Phrases

Can you help me?
Yes, I can help you.
No, I can't help you.
What do you want me to do?

Right away. (Am.)/Straightaway. (Brit.)

Help me please!
Can you give me a hand?
See you soon.
Hugs

SMART TIPS

- It's common to say *Hi!* or *Hello!* when greeting someone. When leaving someone, it's common to say *See you soon!* or *See you later!*

- To politely say that you can't or don't want to help someone, add the following expressions: *No, I'm sorry. I can't help you, I'm afraid.*

Activity A

What do you say when you want to…

1   …ask someone to help you?

    Can you give me a hand?

2   …say that you can't help someone?

    _____

3   …ask someone what he wants you do to?

    _____

4   …say that you will do something immediately?

    _____

Activity B

Put the phrases in the correct order to create a dialogue.

Yes, I can help you. What do you want me to do?

#

Make the bed.

#

Right away.

#

Can you help me?

1

Present and future conditional sentences

Conditional sentences describe a condition (situation) and its results.

Present conditionals describe what usually happens when a condition takes place: *If my apartment is messy, I clean it. If my apartment is messy* is the condition (sometimes my apartment is tidy, not messy). When it's messy, what's the result? *I clean it.*

In present conditionals, the condition starts with *If +* subject + verb in the simple present tense. The result is also in the simple present tense: *If my friends come over to my house, I offer them something to eat.*

Future conditionals describe what will happen if a condition takes place in the future: *If it rains tomorrow, I will stay home.* Will it rain tomorrow? I don't know yet.

In future conditionals, the condition starts with *If +* subject + verb in the simple present tense, but it describes the future, not the present. The result is in the simple future tense: *If my family visits me next weekend, I'll ask them to help me paint my house.*

Activity A

Do the sentences describe present or future conditionals?

1   If I'm sick, I stay in my bedroom all day.

   ⓐ present   **b future**

2   If John doesn't help Elizabeth, she'll be angry.

   a present   **b future**

3   If I have time, I'll clean my kitchen.

   a present   **b future**

4   If Shelly has time in the morning, she makes her bed.

   a present   **b future**

The imperative

The imperative gives orders and instructions. It is formed in English with the verb in its base form. The understood subject *you* (sing. or pl.) is not stated: *Make your bed! Clean up your room!*

For negative imperatives, place *Do not (Don't)* before the verb: *Don't worry! Don't leave your clothes on the floor!*

Activity B

Irina needs help in her house. She asks her family to help. Use the given verb and noun to write each command.

Organize your closet!
organize/your closet

paint/the wall

pick up/your clothes

clean/the floor

LESSON 5
Where did you go?

Diary Entry
Read the following page from Jenny's diary.

> I had a very good week.
> The day before yesterday, my friends and I went to a rock concert. We had a lot of fun. Yesterday, my mother and I went shopping to buy some clothes. Then I went to a nightclub with my boyfriend and we danced all night. I hope we go dancing again very soon!

the day before yesterday	again
We had fun.	very soon
all night	then

Activity A
Circle the correct answer.

1 What did Jenny do the day before yesterday?
   a She went to a concert.
   b She went to a nightclub.

2 What did Jenny do yesterday?
   a She went to a concert.
   b She went shopping.

3 What did Jenny do last night?
   a She went to a concert.
   b She went to a nightclub.

4 What does Jenny want to do again?
   a go shopping   **b** go dancing

Activity B
Answer the questions using complete sentences.

1 What kind of concert did Jenny and her friends go to?
   They went to a rock concert.

2 Did they have a good time at the concert?
   _____

3 When did Jenny go shopping?
   _____

4 What did Jenny do after going shopping?
   _____

Activity C
Write what Jenny did each day.

1 the day before yesterday
   _____

2 yesterday
   _____

3 last night
   _____

SMART TIPS

- In future conditionals, use *will* when you are 100% sure about the result, and use the modals *may* or *might* when you are about 50% sure of the result: *If Jenny isn't tired tomorrow night, she may go out dancing, or she may stay home.*

- In conditionals the condition can come first, or the result can come first. If the condition comes first, remember to use a comma:

  If I have time on weekends, I go out with my friends.
  I go out with my friends if I have time on weekends.
  If I go out with Jane next Saturday night, I'll have a good time.
  I'll have a good time if I go out with Jane next Saturday night.

Words to Know

Essential Words

bar (nightclub)
concert
to dance
movie (Am.)/film (Brit.)
movie theater (Am.)/cinema (Brit.)
theater (Am.)/theatre (Brit.)
day before yesterday
last night
last week
tomorrow
yesterday

Activity A

Where did the people go last night? Choose the correct place for each picture.

1 _____a nightclub_____

2 _____

3 _____

4 _____

Activity B

Today is Wednesday. Write *last night, yesterday, the day before yesterday* or *last week* to say when you did each activity.

1 On Tuesday, I danced. _____*yesterday*_____

2 On Monday, I saw a movie. _____

3 Last Wednesday, I went to a concert.

   _____

4 On Tuesday evening, I went to a bar. _____

Activity C

Write about what you did each day.

1 yesterday

   _____

   _____

2 last night

   _____

   _____

3 the day before yesterday

   _____

   _____

4 last Thursday

   _____

   _____

CULTURE TIP

In the United States, you go to see a *movie* at a *movie theater* and often simply say *the movies: Last night we went to the movies.* In Great Britain, you go to the *pictures* or to the *cinema* to see a *film.*

Smart Phrases

Essential Phrases

What did you do…
  last night?
  last week?
  the day before yesterday?
  yesterday?
What do you want to do?
I want to go out.
I want to stay in.
I want to watch television/TV.

Let's go out.
Let's have a drink.

Activity A

What do you say when you want to…

1 …ask someone what he or she did last week?
   What did you do last week?
   _____

2 …ask someone what he or she wants to do?
   _____

3 …say that you want to go out?
   _____

4 …say that you want to stay home?
   _____

CULTURE TIP

Like many big cities around the world, London and New York are known for their nightlife. New York is called "the city that never sleeps." Indeed, there are lots of places to go: movie theaters, theaters (to see live plays), nightclubs, bars, sports arenas, concert halls and even supermarkets that never close!

London doesn't sleep either, and nightlife there is just as varied and exciting.

Activity B

Ed asks Janet if she wants to go out this evening, but Janet doesn't want to. Ed suggests different activities, but Janet doesn't like any of his ideas. Put the sentences in the correct order to create a dialogue.

___ **Ed** Well, I don't want to stay home. Do you want to go dancing?

___ **Janet** We went to the movies yesterday.

_1_ **Ed** Let's go to the movies.

___ **Janet** I want to stay home tonight.

___ **Ed** OK, we'll stay home tonight.

___ **Janet** I went dancing with my friends last night.

___ **Ed** Well, what do you want to do this evening?

What does Ed finally decide to do tonight?

_____

Activity C

Answer the questions.

1 Do you prefer to go out or stay in on weeknights?
   _____

2 Do you prefer to go out or stay in on weekends?
   _____

3 Do you prefer to go to concerts or nightclubs?
   _____

4 Do you prefer to watch TV or go to the movies?
   _____

Your Turn

What do you want to do tonight?

_____

_____

LESSON 8
Smart Grammar

The past progressive tense

The past progressive verb tense describes actions that were taking place (were in progress) at a specific time in the past: *Jenny and her friend were dancing at a nightclub at 10:30 Saturday night.*

The simple past tense describes actions that ended in the past, but the past progressive describes actions that were still happening in the past: *I was reading a book at 8:30 last night. I started at 7:00 and stopped at 9:00.*

Form the present progressive with *was/were* and the main verb + *-ing*.

Form negative statements by placing *not* before the main verb: *I wasn't (was not) watching a movie at 11:30 last night.*

Form yes/no questions by placing *was/were* before the subject: *Were you cleaning your house when I called you?*

Form information questions by placing a question word before *was/were*: *Why weren't you dancing with your friends last night?*

Remember that only verbs that describe actions can be progressive. Verbs describing states, like *be*, cannot be progressive: *We were at home on Wednesday at 9:30 PM.*

Activity A

Fill in the blanks with the verb in the present progressive tense.

1 We ___*were painting*___ our house Sunday at 3:00.
          paint

2 John _____ the bed when his friends
          make
came over to his house.

3 _____ you _____ television
     watch
at 7:30 PM?

4 Mehmet _____ dinner when Janis
          eat
called him.

Activity B

What were the people doing at 3:00 PM last Tuesday?

Scott

was working.

Katrina and Carl

_____

Mia

_____

Monique

_____

Your Turn

What were you doing yesterday at the following times?

_____

_____

_____

Unit 10 Review

Activity A
Unscramble the letters to form words, using the pictures as clues.

1 m l f i   _f_ _i_ _l_ _m_

2 c d n a e   _ _ _ _ _

3 t a n i p   _ _ _ _ _

4 t h n k i c e   _ _ _ _ _ _ _

5 h m o r b t a o   _ _ _ _ _ _ _ _

Activity B

Match the questions to the correct answers.

1 Do you want to go out tonight?

2 Can you help me, please?

3 What did you do last night?

4 Did you finish cleaning your room

5 Have you ever been to a concert?

6 Do you want to go out tomorrow?

a No, I haven't. I've never seen live music.

b Yes, that's a good idea.

c We went to the movies.

d No, not tonight. I prefer to stay home.

e No, I didn't. I'll clean it tomorrow.

f I'm sorry, I don't have time.

Activity C
Circle the correct answer.

1 Right now I _____ Activity C.
    a am doing   **b** was doing

2 If I _____ time tomorrow, I'll go to the movies.
    a will have   **b** have

3 _____ your bedroom!
    a Clean   **b** You clean

4 I _____ at home at 8:30 last night.
    a was being   **b** was

Activity D
Fill in the blanks with the verb in parentheses in the correct tense.

1 Yesterday we _____*went*_____ to the movies.
                 go

2 Tomorrow I _____ shopping.
                go

3 _____ you _____ in your
                      live
apartment for a long time?

4 I always _____ my bed in the morning.
              make

5 I _____ my house at 11:00 AM last Sunday.
        clean

Challenge
Ask a friend who speaks English what he or she will do next weekend if the weather is nice.

Internet Activity

Go to **www.berlitzpublishing.com** for a list of places where you can talk with English speakers from different countries. Ask them what they did yesterday, last night, the day before yesterday and last week!

In this unit you will learn:
- **vocabulary related to the body and health.**
- **adverbs of time.**
- **to describe the symptoms of common illnesses.**
- **the modal verbs** *should, must* **and** *have to.*

LESSON 1

I'm sick!

Dialogue

Melanie is asking her friend Roberto if he wants to play tennis, but he is sick. They agree to play another day. Listen to their conversation.

Roberto Hi, Melanie. What are you doing today?

Melanie Going to play tennis. Do you want to come?

Roberto No, I can't go out today. I'm sick.

Melanie That's a shame. If you like and if you feel better, we could play on Thursday or Friday?

Roberto Yes, that would be great. If I feel better, we'll play on Friday.

Melanie Good. Call me on Thursday. Take care of yourself!

Activity A

Circle the correct answer.

1 When does Melanie want to play tennis?
   ⓐ today   **b tomorrow**

2 Why doesn't Roberto want to play tennis with Melanie?
   a He doesn't want to.   **b He can't.**

3 When does he want to play?
   a Thursday   **b Friday**

4 Who will call on Thursday?
   a Melanie   **b Roberto**

Activity B

The following Friday, Roberto sends a text message to Melanie. Read his message and Melanie's response. Then answer the questions.

I'm sorry Melanie, I can't play today. I'm still sick. Maybe we could play on Sunday or Monday? Robert

That's a shame, but don't worry. Look after yourself and call me Sunday. Melanie

1 Why can't Roberto play tennis on Friday?
   a He is still sick.   **b He doesn't want to.**

2 What does Melanie tell Roberto in her response?
   a not to call   **b not to worry**

3 When are they going to talk again?
   a Sunday   **b Monday**

Activity C

Today is Sunday. Imagine you are Roberto and are sending a message to Melanie. Tell her that you want to play tennis on Monday.

_____

_____

_____

_____

LESSON 2
Words to Know

Essential Words

Sports

baseball
cycling (bicycle/bike riding)
soccer (Am.)/football (Brit.)
swimming
tennis

Health

fat
gym
healthy
sick (Am.)/ill (Brit.)
slim (thin)
to weigh
weight

Activity A

Write the name of the sport under each picture.

1 _swimming_

3 _____

2 _____

4 _____

Activity B

Look at the Essential Words list. Which sports do you do alone? Which ones do you do with other people?

alone	with other people
	baseball

Your Turn

Which sports to you like to play? Which ones do you like to watch?

SMART TIP

Adjectives describe nouns and adverbs describe verbs: *It was a good* (adj.) *tennis match. We played well* (adv.).

Many adverbs in English are formed by adding *−ly* to an adjective:

slow (adj.) → *slowly* (adv.)
bad (adj.) → *badly* (adv.)
comfortable (adj.) → *comfortably* (adv.)

If an adjective ends in consonant + *−y* change the *−y* to *−i* and then add *−ly* (easy → *easily*). If an adjective ends in *−le*, drop the *−e* and add *−y* (terrible → *terribly*).

If an adjective ends in *−ic*, add *−al* before adding *−ly* (terrific → *terrifically*).

Some adverbs have the same form as the adjective:

fast (adj.) → *fast* (adv.)
hard (adj.) → *hard* (adv.)
late (adj.) → *late* (adv.)

The adjective *good* is irregular: good (adj.) → *well* (adv.)

Smart
Phrases

Essential Phrases

How are you (feeling)?
I'm sick (Am.)/ill (Brit.).
I'm in good health. (I'm healthy.)
I'm not very well./I don't feel very well.
I'm very well.
I want to be in good shape.
I want to gain/put on weight.
I want to lose weight.

I feel better.
I'm sorry.
I think so.

What a shame!

Activity A

What do you say when you want to…

1   …say that you are in good health?

 I'm in good health.

2   …say that you are in good shape?

3   …ask someone how he or she feels?

4   …say that you want to lose weight?

Activity B

Chose the correct phrase for each photo.

1

 ⓐ I'm sick.

 b I'm very well.

2

 a I'm sick.

 b I'm in good shape.

3

 a I'm sick

 b I'm healthy.

4

 a I'm in good health

 b I'm not very well.

Your Turn

How are you? Talk about your health. Use *I'm very well* or *I'm not very well* to say how you are feeling. Then, say if you are *in good* or *bad shape*.

Smart Grammar

Compound Sentences

Compound sentences join two sentences together with a comma and the words *and, but* or *so*.

And introduces additional information: *I went to the gym, and I worked out.*

But introduces different information: *Eduardo likes soccer, but Julio likes baseball.*

So introduces a result: *Jeong Ho went to the gym a lot, so he lost weight.*

Activity A

Circle the correct answer.

1 Li Chuan was sick, _____ she didn't go to work.

   a but   **(b) so**

2 Miguel rides his bicycle every day, _____ Beatriz does too.

   a and   **b but**

3 Amparo wants to gain weight, _____ Alfonso wants to lose weight.

   a but   **b so**

4 Kenny is slim, _____ Charlie is too.

   a and   **b so**

SMART TIP

In a compound sentence, when both verbs are the same, use *do/does/did + too*:

Tammy loves sports, and Sean does too. = *Tammy loves sports, and Sean loves sports too.*

Maggie went to the gym last night, and Paul did too.

When both verbs are a form of *be*, use *am/are/is/was/were + too*:

I am healthy, and you are too. = *I am healthy, and you are healthy too.*

Vinnie was playing tennis at 3:00 PM, and Amelia was too.

Activity B

Combine the two sentences into one compound sentence.

1 Marta loves riding her bicycle. She loves playing tennis.

   Marta loves riding her bicycle, and she loves

   playing tennis.

2 We felt tired. We didn't go to the gym.

   _____

   _____

3 I like soccer. I don't play it very well.

   _____

   _____

4 Simon was bored. He decided to watch baseball on TV.

   _____

   _____

Your Turn

Look at each picture and write a compound sentence about it.

1 *It's going to rain, so you*

   should bring an umbrella.

   _____

2 _____

   _____

   _____

3 _____

   _____

   _____

4 _____

   _____

   _____

LESSON 5
Medicine

Medical Advertisement

Read and listen to these advertisements (ads).

Medicine for colds

Fights coughs and sneezes.

Calms headaches and sore throats.

Brings down your temperature.

Thanks to this medicine, you'll feel better right away.

No need to call the doctor!

You can take this medicine three times a day!

> fight   sneeze
> cough   sore throat

Activity A
Circle the correct answer.

1   What is this ad for?

   a pain medicine   **ⓑ cold medicine**

2   What does this medicine treat?

   a a fever   **b a toothache**

3   What does this medicine calm?

   a toothaches   **b headaches**

4   How many times a day can this medicine be taken?

   a two times   **b three times**

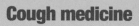

Cough medicine

For fast cough relief.

Brings down your temperature and stops your headache.

Take once a day.

Must have a doctor's prescription!

Feel better right away.

> relief   prescription
> bring down

Activity B
Circle the correct answer.

1   What is this ad for?

   ⓐ cough medicine   **b cold medicine**

2   What does this medicine treat?

   a a fever   **b a toothache**

3   How many times a day can this medicine be taken?

   a once   **b three times**

4   Is it necessary to see a doctor to get this medicine?

   a yes   **b no**

Activity C
Complete the sentences.

Both medicines will bring down your ___temperature___ and calm your _____.

The medicine for colds also fights _____ and _____.

You need a _____ for the cough medicine.

> **SMART TIP**
>
> Sometimes a noun and a verb have the same form:
> *a cough/to cough   a sneeze/to sneeze   a dance/to dance*

Words to Know

Essential Words

cold
cough/to cough
doctor
dentist
to feel sick
headache
hospital
injection/shot
medicine
prescription
sore throat
stomachache
temperature
toothache

Activity A

Circle the correct answer.

1   I have a bad cough. I need to see a _____.

   a dentist   (**b**) **doctor**

2   I have a toothache. I need to go to a _____.

   a hospital   **b** dentist

3   I have a temperature. I want my doctor to give me a(n) _____ to get some medicine.

   a prescription   **b** injection

4   I am very, very sick. My doctor told me to go to the _____.

   a dentist   **b** hospital

Activity B

What is wrong with each person?

1   Antonio *has a stomachache.*

2   Teresa _____

3   Arnaud _____

4   Nina _____

Your Turn

Imagine you are a doctor. Talk about your patients in the pictures above. What do they need?

1   Antonio *needs to stop eating.*

2   Teresa _____

3   Arnaud _____

4   Nina _____

SMART TIP

Should gives advice: *Antonio should stop eating. Arnaud should take an aspirin. Must* is stronger than *should* and expresses that something is necessary: *Nina must go to a dentist! Have/has to* is also used instead of *must: Nina has to go to a dentist!*

Be careful with the negative of *have/has to: Nina doesn't have to go to the dentist.* = Nina can go or not. It's not necessary.

Smart Phrases

Essential Phrases

Where does it hurt?

My arm hurts.

My back hurts.

My hand hurts.

My feet hurt.

My legs hurt.

I have a pain in my foot.

Can you recommend a doctor/dentist?

I need to see a doctor/dentist.

> **SMART TIP**
>
> When a part of the body hurts, use a possessive adjective: *I have a pain in my left side. His leg hurts.*

> **SMART TIP**
>
> Reflexive pronouns are used when the subject and the object are the same (subject = object), and are often used when people hurt themselves. *I cut myself. She hurt herself. They burned themselves. We scratched ourselves.* The reflexive pronouns in English are:
>
> I → myself
> you (sing.) → yourself
> he → himself
> she → herself
> it → itself
> we → ourselves
> you (pl.) → yourselves
> they → themselves

Activity A

Look at each picture and complete the sentence that describes it.

1 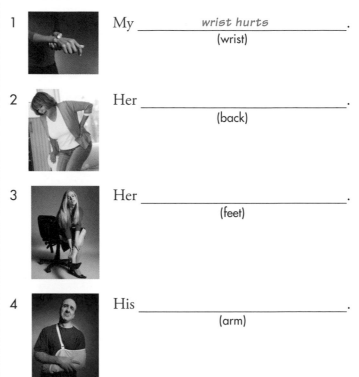 My _____*wrist hurts*_____.
   (wrist)

2 Her _____.
   (back)

3 Her _____.
   (feet)

4 His _____.
   (arm)

Activity B

Complete the sentences with the correct reflexive pronoun.

1 I burned ____*myself*____.

2 She cut _____.

3 We hurt _____.

4 He scratched _____.

5 They hurt _____.

Your Turn

You're waiting to see the doctor. Tell the nurse how you are feeling and describe your symptoms. Use the words below.

temperature	sore throat	pain
stomachache	backache	
headache	cough	

_____

_____

_____

LESSON 8

Smart Grammar

Adverbs of frequency

Adverbs of frequency describe how often an action happens. They usually come between the subject and the verb: *We often go* swimming on Saturdays, or they come between the helping verb and the main verb: *You should always go* to the doctor when you're sick.

Adverbs of frequency come after *be*: *She is seldom sick.*

The most common adverbs of frequency are:

always (100%)
usually (90-99%)
often (75-90%)
sometimes (25-75%)
seldom/rarely (1-25%)
never (0%)

Activity A

Circle **T** for true and **F** for false.

1 Cindy watches baseball on TV every Sunday.
   Cindy rarely watches baseball on TV.   **T /(F)**

2 Elena doesn't know how to speak Hindi.
   Elena never speaks Hindi.   **T / F**

3 Jorge and Ana go to concerts three or four times a year.
   Jorge and Ana always go to concerts.   **T / F**

4 Nigel went to the hospital one time.
   Nigel usually goes to the hospital.   **T / F**

Activity B

Circle the answer that best describes yourself.

1 I'm _____ sick.
   a always   **c** sometimes
   b often   **d** never

2 I _____ play football.
   a always   **c** sometimes
   b often   **d** never

3 I _____ play baseball.
   a always   **c** sometimes
   b often   **d** never

4 I _____ take medicine when I'm sick.
   a always   **c** sometimes
   b often   **d** never

Activity C

Complete the sentences with the correct adverbs of frequency.

1 Byung Jin _____*rarely*_____ sees a doctor when he's sick. (20% of the time)

2 Ethan _____ eats healthy food. (95% of the time)

3 Guadalupe _____ cuts herself when she cooks. (0% of the time).

4 Min-Hsing _____ plays tennis with her friends on Sundays. (80% of the time)

Your Turn

Use the adverbs of frequency to write about some activities in your own life.

1 always _____

   _____

2 usually _____

   _____

3 never _____

   _____

Activity A

Jim and Mick are brothers, but they never agree! If Mick says something, Jim immediately says the opposite. Fill in the blanks of the dialogue with the opposite of what Jim says.

Jim I want to lose weight.

Mick *I want to gain weight.* _____

Jim I'm in bad shape.

Mick _____

Jim I feel better.

Mick _____

Jim I never take medicine.

Mick _____

Activity B

What's wrong with these sentences? Rewrite them so that they are correct.

1 I have headache.

   I have a headache. _____

2 I have played tennis yesterday.

   _____

3 She plays baseball good.

   _____

4 Ourselves exercise a lot.

   _____

5 I hurt himself.

   _____

6 They go never swimming.

   _____

Activity C

Unscramble the letters to form words, using the pictures as clues.

1 n y l c i c g   _C_ _Y_ _C_ _L_ _I_ _N_ _G_

2 s e n t i n   _ _ _ _ _ _

3 e c a h d a e h   _ _ _ _ _ _ _ _

4 n m i c e d e i   _ _ _ _ _ _ _ _

5 e t p e u r m e a t r   _ _ _ _ _ _ _ _ _ _ _

6 n s t i t e d   _ _ _ _ _ _ _

Challenge

Answer the following questions about yourself.

What sports do you usually play?

_____

When was the last time you were sick?

_____

What do you do when you have a cough?

_____

Internet Activity

Go to **www.berlitzpublishing.com** for a list of gyms in Great Britain and in the United States. Chose a gym and find out what you can do there. How can you become a member? What kind of equipment and activities do they propose? Can you take dance classes there?

Numbers

0	zero
1	one
2	two
3	three
4	four
5	five
6	six
7	seven
8	eight
9	nine
10	ten
11	eleven
12	twelve
13	thirteen
14	fourteen
15	fifteen
16	sixteen
17	seventeen
18	eighteen
19	nineteen
20	twenty
21	twenty-one
22	twenty-two
23	twenty-three
24	twenty-four
25	twenty-five
26	twenty-six
27	twenty-seven
28	twenty-eight
29	twenty-nine
30	thirty
40	forty
50	fifty
60	sixty
70	seventy
80	eighty
90	ninety
100	one hundred
101	one hundred and one
200	two hundred
500	five hundred

1,000	one thousand
10,000	ten thousand
100,000	one hundred thousand
1,000,000	one million

Days

Sunday
Monday
Tuesday
Wednesday
Thursday
Friday
Saturday

Months

January
February
March
April
May
June
July
August
September
October
November
December

Countries/Nationalities

Australia
Australian

Germany
German

Belgium
Belgian

Haiti
Haitian

Brazil
Brazilian

India
Indian

Cameroon
Cameroonian

Indonesia
Indonesian

Canada
Canadian

Ireland
Irish

China
Chinese

Italy
Italian

Colombia
Colombian

Korea
Korean

El Salvador
Salvadoran

Mexico
Mexican

France
French

New Zealand
New Zealander

Countries/Nationalities

Pakistan
Pakistani

Philippines
Filipino (m.)/Filipina (f.)

Portugal
Portuguese

Russia
Russian

Senegal
Senegalese

South Africa
South African

Spain
Spanish

Switzerland
Swiss

Thailand
Thai

Turkey
Turkish

United Kingdom
English

United States
American

Vietnam
Vietnamese

Colors

■ black

■ purple

■ blue

■ red

■ brown

□ white

■ green

□ yellow

■ pink

Clothing Sizes

Women's Dresses		Men's Shirts	
USA	UK	USA	UK
4	6	14	14
6	8	14½	14½
8	10	15	15
10	12	15½	15½
12	14	16	16
14	16	16½	16½
16	18	17	17

Women's Shoes		Men's Shoes	
USA	UK	USA	UK
5	2½	6	5½
6	3½	7	6½
7	4½	8	7½
8	5½	9	8½
9	6½	10	9½
10	7½	11	10½
11	8½	12	11½
12	9½	13	12½

Seasons

 fall/autumn

winter

 summer

 spring

Common Noncount Nouns

bread	baseball	work
cake	football	homework
cereal	soccer	housework
cheese	tennis	
chicken		
fish	cycling	
food	swimming	
fruit		
ice cream	reading	
meat	shopping	
pie	traveling	
rice		
salt	cash	
pepper	change	
	money	
beer		
coffee	clothing	
juice	health	
milk	information	
soup	luggage	
tea	transportation	
water	weather	
wine		

Common Non-Action (Stative) Verbs

be	feel	hate	believe	cost
look*	hear	like	forget	have**
seem	see	love	know	own
	smell	need	remember	
	taste	want	think	
		understand		

* *look* is a non-action verb when it means *seem*:
You *look/seem* tired today.
look is an action verb when it's used with *for* and *at*:
Karen was *looking for* her cat this morning.
She finally found her cat, and now she's *looking at* him.

** *have* is a non-action verb when it means *own*:
Victoria *has/owns* two cars.
have is an action verb when it means *eat* or *drink*:
I'm *having/drinking* coffee right now.

Spelling Rules

Regular Plural Nouns and Third Person Singular (he, she, it) Simple Present Tense

Add –s for most nouns and verbs:
house → houses   car → cars
eat → eats   buy → buys

Add –es for nouns and verbs that end in –s, –x, –z, –ch, –sh:
bus → buses   box → boxes   church → churches   dish → dishes
miss → misses   fax → faxes   buzz → buzzes   catch → catches   wash → washes

Change –y to –i and add –es for nouns and verbs that end in a consonant + -y:

baby → babies   cherry → cherries
study → studies   fly → flies

Change to –ves nouns that end in –fe and –lf :
knife → knives   life → lives

Present and Past Progressive (–ing)

Add –ing for most verbs:
talk → talking   eat → eating

Drop –e before adding –ing:
make → making   leave → leaving

Change –ie to –y before adding –ing:
lie → lying   die → dying

Double the consonant for one-syllable verbs that end in a vowel + a consonant:
stop → stopping   sit → sitting

Don't double the consonant if the verb ends in –w, -x or –y:
show → showing   mix → mixing
play → playing

Double the consonant for verbs with two or more syllables that end in a vowel
+a consonant and the last syllable is stressed:
begin → beginning   occur → occurring

Don't double the consonant if the verb ends in –w, -x or -y:
allow → allowing   remix → remixing
obey → obeying

Regular Simple Past Tense Verbs (-ed)

Add –ed for most verbs:
watch → watched   talk → talked

Add –d for verbs that end in –e:
live → lived   lie → lied

Change –y to –i for verbs that end in a consonant + –y:
try → tried   study → studied

Double the consonant for one-syllable verbs that end in a vowel + a consonant:
stop → stopped

Don't double the consonant if the verb ends in –w, –x or –y:
show → showed   mix → mixed   play → played

Double the consonant for verbs with two or more syllables that end in a vowel + a consonant and the last syllable is stressed:
permit → permitted   occur → occurred

Don't double the consonant if the verb ends in –w, –x or –y:
allow → allowed   remix → remixed   obey → obeyed

Irregular Verbs

Base Form	Simple Past	Past Participle
arise	arose	arisen
awake	awoke	awoken
be	was/were	been
beat	beat	beaten
become	became	become
begin	began	begun
bend	bent	bent
bet	bet	bet
bite	bit	bitten
blow	blew	blown
break	broke	broken
bring	brought	brought
build	built	built
burn	burned/burnt	burned/burnt
buy	bought	bought
catch	caught	caught
choose	chose	chosen
come	came	come
cost	cost	cost
creep	crept	crept
cut	cut	cut
dig	dug	dug
dive	dived/dove	dived
do	did	done
draw	drew	drawn
dream	dreamed/dreamt	dreamed/dreamt
drink	drank	drunk
drive	drove	driven
eat	ate	eaten
fall	fell	fallen
feed	fed	fed
feel	felt	felt
fight	fought	fought
find	found	found
fit	fit	fit

Base Form	Simple Past	Past Participle
flee	fled	fled
fling	flung	flung
fly	flew	flown
forbid	forbade/forbad	forbidden
forget	forgot	forgotten
forgive	forgave	forgiven
freeze	froze	frozen
get	got	gotten/got
give	gave	given
go	went	gone
grow	grew	grown
hang	hung	hung
have	had	had
hear	heard	heard
hide	hid	hidden
hit	hit	hit
hold	held	held
hurt	hurt	hurt
keep	kept	kept
kneel	knelt	knelt
knit	knit/knitted	knit/knitted
know	knew	known
lay	laid	laid
lead	led	led
leap	leapt	leapt
leave	left	left
lend	lent	lent
let	let	let
lie	lay	lain
light	lit/lighted	lit/lighted
lose	lost	lost
make	made	made
mean	meant	meant
meet	met	met
pay	paid	paid
prove	proved	proved/proven
put	put	put

Base Form	Simple Past	Past Participle
quit	quit	quit
read	read	read
ride	rode	ridden
ring	rang	rung
rise	rose	risen
run	ran	ran
say	said	said
see	saw	seen
seek	sought	sought
sell	sold	sold
send	sent	sent
set	set	set
sew	sewed	sewn/sewed
shake	shook	shaken
shave	shaved	shaved/shaven
shoot	shot	shot
show	showed	shown
shrink	shrink/shrank	shrunk/shrunken
shut	shut	shut
sing	sang	sung
sink	sank	sunk
sit	sat	sat
sleep	slept	slept
slide	slid	slid
speak	spoke	spoken
speed	sped	sped
spend	spent	spent
spill	spilled/spilt	spilled/split
spin	spun	spun
spit	spit/spat	spat
split	split	split
spread	spread	spread
spring	sprang	sprung
stand	stood	stood
steal	stole	stolen
stick	stuck	stuck
sting	stung	stung
strike	struck	struck

Base Form	Simple Past	Past Participle
swear	swore	sworn
sweep	swept	swept
swim	swam	swum
swing	swung	swung
take	took	taken
teach	taught	taught
tear	torn	torn
tell	told	told
think	thought	thought
throw	threw	thrown
understand	understood	understood
upset	upset	upset
wake	woke	woken
wear	worn	worn
weep	wept	wept
win	won	won
wind	wound	wound
withdraw	withdrew	withdrawn
write	wrote	written

Unit 1 Lesson 1

Activity A 1 T; 2 T; 3 F; 4 T

Activity B

My name is Lisa. What's your name?; My name's Jake. Nice to meet you.; I'm from England. Where are you from?; I'm from the United States.

Lesson 2

Activity A

1 Hello!/Hi!,; 2 What is/What's your name?; 3 Where are you from?; 4 Goodbye!/Bye!; 5 I am/I'm sorry. I have to go.

Activity B

1 Good afternoon!; 2 Good night!; 3 Good morning!

Lesson 3

Activity A

Europe, left to right: 1; 2
North America, top to bottom: 4; 3

Activity B

From left to right: 4; 1; 3; 2

Lesson 4

Activity A

1 I; 2 she; 3 he; 4 you

Activity B

1 they; 2 they; 3 you

Activity C

1 I; 2 she; 3 he; 4 they; 5 they

Lesson 5

Activity A

language: English, English
nationality: American, British

Activity B

1 a; 2 a; 3 b; 4 b

Lesson 6

Activity A

1 Canadian; 2 Mexican; 3 Indian; 4 Vietnamese

Activity B

1 Spanish; 2 Italian; 3 English; 4 American; 5 French

Lesson 7

Activity A

1 I'm French.; 2 Are you English?; 3 I don't speak English very well.; 4 I speak very little English.

Your Turn

Question 1 : Where are you from?
Answer 1 : I'm from Great Britain.
Question 2 : What language do you speak?
Answer 2 : I speak English.

Lesson 8

Activity A

1 am; 2 is; 3 are; 4 is

Activity B

1 are; 2 are; 3 are; 4 are

Activity C

Raphaël	Where are you from?
Jane	I'm from England. Are you Spanish?
Raphaël	I'm French and Paloma is Mexican.

Review

Activity A

Name	Country	Nationality
Pierre	France	French
Cassandra	Canada	Canadian
Brian	the United States	American
Katie	England	English
Paloma	Spain	Spanish

Activity B

1 Laura is English.; 2 Carlos and Marta are Colombian.; 3 Manmohan is Indian.; 4 You're Canadian.; 5 Terre is Australian.

Activity C

Guide	Hello! Welcome to the United States!
Javier	Hello! My name's/I'm Javier. What's your name?
Guide	My name's/I'm Joe. Nice to meet you.
Javier	Nice to meet you too. Are you American?
Guide	Yes. And where are you from?
Javier	I'm from Mexico. Do you speak Spanish?
Guide	A little.
Javier	I'm sorry, my English is not very good.
Guide	No, your English is very good!

Activity D

V K C X U P I N D I A D C N M K
K R U S A Y J S J Y B V A G L R
O O A I X X B P B A Y M N R I J
R S A U S T R A L I A N A Q C E
E R M V G W Q I W E J T D A F Z
A X Z V G N D N I R E L A N D F
P D V S U Q K M E X S P M Z Z W
G E A Y A D B L S F Q Z U Z W O

Challenge

North America: North American; South America: South American

Activity E

1 Hello! My name is Laura.; 2 We are from Canada.; 3 John is from England. He is English.; 4 Mei is from China.; 5 I speak English.; 6 We are from the Philippines.

Unit 2 Lesson 1

Activity A

1 F; 2 F; 3 T; 4 T

Activity B

1 boys; girls; men; women 2 houses; buildings; cars; taxis 3 cats; dogs

Your Turn

Answers will vary.

Lesson 2

Activity A

1 a- a girl; b- a boy; c- a woman; d- a man.
2 a- a man; b- a bus; c- a dog; d- a boy; e- a house; f- a cat; g- a woman; h- a car

Activity B

1 a; 2 a; 3 a; 4 an; 5 an; 6 a; 7 an; 8 a

Lesson 3

Activity A

1 Look at the people!; 2 Look at the animals!

Activity B

Answers may vary. Possible answers:
Dear Marta, I'm having a great time here, and I'm learning a little English. Turn over my postcard and look at the streets! There's a taxi. Look at the typical buildings and the people! I miss you. Blanca

Lesson 4

Activity A

1 men; 2 women; 3 children; 4 houses

Activity B

1 the; 2 –; 3 the; 4 the; 5 the; 6 – '

Lesson 5

Activity A

1 Jameson; 2 June 30, 1978; 3 Akron, Ohio; 4 2017

Activity B

Answers will vary.

Lesson 6

Activity A

fifteen, sixteen, seventeen, eighteen, nineteen, twenty, twenty-one, twenty-two, twenty-three, twenty-four, twenty-five, twenty-six, twenty-seven, twenty-eight, twenty-nine, thirty

Activity B

1 one; 6 six; 13 thirteen; 18 eighteen; 10 ten; 30 thirty; 4 four; 9 nine; 12 twelve; 15 fifteen; 22 twenty two; 14 fourteen

Activity C

1 11; 2 21 Harvey Street; 3 7183754219; 4 58296

Lesson 7

Activity A

Answers will vary.

Activity B

1 a; 2 a; 3 a; 4 b

Lesson 8

Activity A

	Affirmative	Negative	Question
I	work	don't work	Do I work?
you	work	don't work	Do you work?
he/she/it	works	doesn't work	Does he/she/it work?
we	work	don't work	Do we work?
you	work	don't work	Do you work?
they	work	don't work	Do they work?

Activity B

1 visit; 2 is speaking; 3 am working; 4 study; 5 like; 6 is reading

Review

Activity A

1 three boys; 2 one house; 3 two telephones/phones/cell phones; 4 five girls

Activity B

1 Andrew lives at 8 Sixth Avenue.; 2 Sally's phone number is four-eight-two nine-one-three seven-three-nine-one.; 3 Corrine and Mark live at 30 Little Road.; 4 Andrew's phone number is four-four two-zero two-two-seven-eight three-six-two-five.; 4 Sally lives at 25 Huron Street.

Activity C

1 a; 2 an; 3 a; 4 some

Activity D

Answers will vary.
My name is…; My phone number is…; My address is…; My zip code is…; My date of birth is…; Thank you!

Unit 3 Lesson 1

Activity A

1 It's half past six.; 2 It ends in twenty five-minutes.; 3 It lasts forty-eight minutes.; 4 Knicks 48, Bulls 42.

Activity B

1 What time is it?; 2 It's half past six.; 3 It's early! When does the game end?; 4 It ends in twenty-five minutes.

Lesson 2

Activity A

1 It's early!; 2 It's late!; 3 It's early!; 4 It's late!

Activity B

1 It's a quarter past seven.; 2 It's a quarter to four.; 3 It's a quarter past one.; 4 It's six thirty.; 5 It's a quarter past ten.

Lesson 3

Activity A

1 forty-four; 2 thirty-two; 3 sixty-seven; 4 fifty-eight

Activity B

1 It ends in one hour and fifteen minutes.; 2 It ends in two hours.; 2 It ends in five minutes.; 3 It ends in one hour and forty five minutes.; 4 It ends in half an hour.

Your Turn

Answers will vary.
I usually wake up at…; I usually eat breakfast at…; I usually go to work/school at …; I usually go to bed at…

Lesson 4

Activity A

1 on; 2 behind; 3 between

Activity B

1 around; 2 out of; 3 past

Lesson 5

Activity A

1 a; 2 b; 3 a; 4 b

Activity B

1 Julia has to do her homework.; 2 Julia has to call Carlos.; 3 Julia has to do the laundry.; 4 Julia has to exercise.

Lesson 6

Activity A

1 Tuesday; 2 Monday and Thursday; 3 Friday; 4 Wednesday and Saturday; 5 Sunday

Activity B

1 Thursday, February 24th; 2 Monday, November 17th; 3 Saturday, June 5th; 4 Wednesday, September 21st; 5 Friday, April 3rd; 6 Tuesday, January 31st; 7 Sunday, October 12th; 8 Thursday, March 25th; 9 Sunday, August 22nd

Lesson 7

Activity A

1 b; 2 b; 3 a; 4 b

Activity B

1 What day is today?; 2 What's the date today?; 3 What month is it?; 4 What year is it?

Lesson 8

Activity A

1 c; 2 a; 3 b

Activity B

1 He is making a cake.; 2 Lucio is doing the gardening.; 3 Sheila is doing the laundry.; 4 Jane and Betty are making a decision.; 5 Isabella is making tea.; 6 Li is making the bed.; 7 Abdul and Badra are doing homework.; 8 Cynthia is making a phone call.; 9 Khanh is doing the dishes.; 10 Paul is doing housework.; 11 Janis is making a mistake.

Your Turn

Answers will vary.

Review

Activity A

Answers may vary. Possible answers:
1 She does her homework at twelve thirty.; 2 She washes the clothes at a quarter to nine/eight forty-five.; 3 She sweeps the floor at six o'clock.; 4 She exercises at a quarter to eight.; 5 She calls Julia at a quarter past eleven.

Activity B

1 It ends in one hour, thirty one minutes and two seconds.; 2 It ends in two hours, thirty four minutes and thirteen seconds.; 3 It ends in twenty seven seconds.; 4 It ends in twelve minutes and thirty nine seconds.

Activity C

1 Tuesday, February 23rd; 2 Wednesday, February 3rd; 3 Thursday, February 18th; 4 Saturday, February 13th.; 5 Monday, February 15th

Challenge

Answers will vary.

Unit 4 Lesson 1

Activity A

1 F; 2 T; 3 F; 4 F

Activity B

1 a; 2 a; 3 b; 4 b; 5 b

Lesson 2

Activity A

1 family; 2 father; 3 mother; 4 sister; 5 husband.

Activity B

1 brother; 2 sister; 3 mother; 4 father; 5 parents; 6 son; 7 daughter; 8 children; 9 wife; 10 husband

Lesson 3

Activity A

1 Do you have a big family?
2 Yes, I have a big family. And do you have a big family?
3 No. My family is small. I just have one sister.
4 I've got three brothers and two sisters. Look at this photo.
5 What a big family!

Activity B

1 It's a small family.; 2 It's a big family.; 3 It's a big family.; 4 It's a small family.

Your Turn

Answers will vary.

Lesson 4

Activity A

1 my; 2 your; 3 Their; 4 my; 5 your; 6 her; 7 His; 8 our

Activity B

1 e; 2 b; 3 d; 4 c; 5 f; 6 a

Lesson 5

Activity A

1 grandfather; 2 parents; 3 cousin; 4 niece

Activity B

1 mother; 2 cousin; 3 grandmother; 4 nephew

Lesson 6

Activity A

1 T; 2 F; 3 F; 4 T

Activity B

1 a; 2 b; 3 b; 4 a; 5 b; 6 b

Lesson 7

Activity A

1 d; 2 a; 3 c; 4 b; 5 e

Activity B

1 Do you have any cousins?; 2 Do you have any uncles?; 3 Do you have any nephews? 4 Do you have any brothers (and sisters)?

Your Turn

Answers will vary.

Lesson 8

Activity A

1 b; 2 a; 3 a; 4 b; 5 a

Activity B

1 He has an uncle.; 2 My uncle has some nieces.; 3 I have a sister-in-law.; 4 She has some brothers.

Your Turn

Answers will vary.

Review

Activity A

Janet   That's my grandfather, Alfie. And that's my grandmother, Diane.
Paul   And who is that girl?
Janet   That's my cousin, Penelope, and that's my cousin, Mike.
Paul   Is that lady your mother?
Janet   No, she's my aunt, Connie. Penelope and Mike are her step-children.
Paul   Who's that woman?
Janet: She's Linda, my mother.

Activity B

1 her aunt; 2 her mother; 3 her cousins; 4 her grandparents.

Challenge

Do you have any brothers and sisters? Do you have a lot of cousins? Do you have any nieces or nephews?

Activity C

Paul   Is this/that boy your nephew?
Alfie   No, he's my grandson.
Paul   Who are these/those children?
Alfie   They are my grandchildren.
Paul   Is this/that man your son?
Alfie   No, he's my nephew! These/Those men are my sons.

Activity D

1 There are two children.; 2 There are three children.; 3 There are two children.; 4 There is one child.

Unit 5 Lesson 1

Activity A

1 T; 2 T; 3 F; 4 F

Activity B

1 a; 2 b; 3 b; 4 b

Lesson 2

Activity A

1 fruit; 2 coffee; 3 cereal; 4 beer

Your Turn

Answers will vary.

Lesson 3

Activity A

1 I'm hungry.; 2 I'm thirsty.; 3 I'm hungry.; 4 I'm thirsty.; 5 I'm hungry.; 6 I'm thirsty.

Activity B

1 I'd like; 2 I'd fancy; 3 I'd fancy; 4 I'd like

Activity C 1 breakfast; 2 lunch; 3 dinner

Lesson 4

Activity A

1 Where; 2 What; 3 When; 4 Which; 5 Who

Activity B

1 a; 2 b; 3 a; 4 a

Activity C 1 why; 2 who; 3 when; 4 where

Your Turn

1 What's your mother's name?; 2 What time is it?; 3 Who are they?; 4 Where does she live?

Lesson 5

Activity A

1 a; 2 b; 3 b; 4 a

Activity B

2; 3; 1; 4

Lesson 6

Activity A

1 appetizer; 2 main course; 3 dessert; 4 main course

Activity B

1 The bruschetta is an appetizer.; 2 The steak/meat is a main course.; 3 The cake is a dessert.

Your Turn

Answers will vary.

Lesson 7

Activity A

1 Enjoy your meal.; 2 Could/Can I have the bill, please?; 3 Could/Can I see the wine list, please?; 4 My food tastes really good.

Activity B

1 b; 2 a; 3 b; 4 a

Your Turn

Answers will vary.

Lesson 8

Activity A

1 a; 2 b; 3 a; 4 a

Activity B

1 permission; 2 request; 3 request; 4 permission

Your Turn

Answers will vary.

Review

Activity A

1 has; 2 is; 3 are; 4 are; 5 have; 6 have; 7 is; 8 are

Activity B

Appetizers: Soup, Shrimp cocktail

Main course: Burger and fries, Chicken with rice

Dessert: Apple pie, Chocolate cake

Activity C

Bill	I'm hungry.
Angela	What would you like to eat?
Bill	I'd like some chicken.
Angela	Let's go to a restaurant.
Bill	Where is the restaurant?
Angela	It's that way.
Angela	What would you like for the main course?
Bill	I'd like chicken.
Angela	Waiter, can I have the check/bill, please?

Challenge

Answers will vary.

Unit 6 Lesson 1

Activity A

1 It's five degrees Celsius.; 2 It's fifty degrees Fahrenheit.; 3 It's cold and sunny.; 4 It's windy and it's raining.

Activity B

1 It's twenty degrees Fahrenheit.; 2 It's sixty-seven degrees Celsius.; 3 It's eighty-five degrees Fahrenheit.; 4 It's twenty-nine degrees Celsius.

Lesson 2

Activity A

1 c; 2 d; 3 a; 4 b

Activity B

1 a; 2 b; 3 b; 4 b

Activity C

Answers will vary.

Lesson 3

Activity A

What's the temperature? 35°C, 65°F, 20°C
What's the weather like? It's raining., It's warm., It's cold.

Activity B 1 b; 2 d; 3 a; 4 c

Activity C 1 a; 2 a; 3 b; 4 a

Lesson 4

Activity A

1 d; 2 c; 3 a; 4 b; 5 e

Activity B 1 a big red ball; 2 a beautiful sunny day; 3 a tall young boy; 4 a fast French car

Your Turn
Answers will vary.

Lesson 5

Activity A

summer activities: plays soccer, swims, runs
winter clothes: a hat, a scarf, a coat, gloves

Activity B

1 plays soccer; 2 the U.S.; 3 summer; 4 winter

Lesson 6

Activity A

Answers may vary. Possible answers:
1 It's fun.; 2 It's fun.; 3 It's boring; 4 It's boring.

Activity B

1 What are you doing?; 2 What do you usually do in the summer?; 3 I usually…in the winter.; 4 That's right./You're right.

Your Turn Answers will vary.

Lesson 7

Activity A 1 shoes; 2 gloves; 3 hat; 4 jacket

Activity B 1 fall; 2 spring; 3 winter; 4 summer

Activity C

1 hat, coat, gloves, scarf, shoes; 2 jacket, shoes; 3 hat, sandals, shorts; 4 jacket, shoes

Lesson 8

Activity A 1 worked; 2 played; 3 liked; 4 looked

Activity B

1 Did they walk to school?; 2 Did they finish their homework?; 3 Did they need some money?; 4 Did she call?

Activity C

1 No, I didn't finish the cake.; 2 Yes, she called John.; 3 No, they didn't speak English.; 4 Yes, they waited for me.; 5 No, he didn't need to leave.; 6 Yes, they walked here.

Review

Activity A It's raining.; 2 It's cold.; 3 It's windy; 4 It's cloudy

Activity B

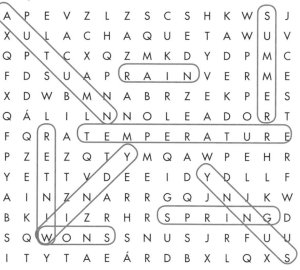

Activity C 1 What does it feel like?; 2 What does it taste like?; 3 What does it smell like?; 4 What does it look like?

Activity D

Yes, I invited them.; No, I didn't call Leslie.; Did I finish cooking the food?

Challenge
Answers will vary.

Unit 7 Lesson 1

Activity A

1 c; 2 b; 3 b

Activity B

1 Can I help you?; 2 What size are you looking for?; 3 And which color would you like?; 4 Would you like to try it on?

Lesson 2

Activity A

1 a; 2 a; 3 a; 4 a

Activity B

1 I'm looking for a shirt.; 2 I need a medium, please.; 3 I want to buy a coat.; 4 I'd like a red coat, please.

Lesson 3

Activity A

1 t-shirt; 2 pants; 3 dress; 4 shirt; 5 skirt

Activity B

1 a; 2 b; 3 a; 4 a

Lesson 4

Activity A

1 on; 2 on; 3 out; 4 off

Activity B

1 many; 2 much; 3 many; 4 much; 5 many

Activity C

1 Yes, but I don't have much.; 2 Yes, but I don't have much.; 3 Yes, but I don't have many.; 4 Yes, but I don't have much.; 5 Yes, but I don't have many.; 6 Yes, but I don't have many.

Lesson 5

Activity A

1 b; 2 a; 3 b

Activity B

1 a; 2 b; 3 b; 4 a

Lesson 6

Activity A

1 Do you take credit cards?; 2 How much is the/this/that skirt?; 3 Do you accept checks?; 4 I'm going to pay with a credit card.; 5 How much is the/this/that pair of pants?; 6 I want to buy a skirt.

Activity B

1 expensive; 2 cheap; 3 expensive; 4 cheap

Lesson 7

Activity A

1 checks; 2 credit card; 3 receipt

Activity B

Pooja	I want to buy those dresses but I don't have much money. How about you?
James	I don't have much money but I've got five credit cards.
Pooja	Really? I haven't got many credit cards but I've got some cash and a check book.
James	How much cash do you have?
Pooja	I have $78 in cash.
James	Good. I think we have enough to pay for some dresses. How many dresses do you want?

Your Turn

Answers will vary.

Lesson 8

Activity A

1 more than; 2 less than; 3 less than; 4 more than

Activity B

1 anyone; 2 Someone; 3 anything; 4 anything

Review

Activity A

Simon	Hello, I'd like to look at that blue shirt. How much is it, please? And do you have the shirt in any other color?
Salesperson	It's $25. Yes, we have several colors.
Simon	How many colors do you have?
Salesperson	There are four colors. Red, yellow, blue and green.
Simon	I'd like two green shirts, three blue shirts and one red shirt, please!
Salesperson	Sorry, how many blue shirts do you want?
Simon	I want three, please.
Salesperson	That's a lot of shirts. Are they for you?
Simon	No, they're for my cousins. How much is that altogether, please?
Salesperson	That's $150, please. How would you like to pay?
Simon	With a credit card.

Activity B

1 The t-shirt costs less than the skirt./The skirt costs more than the t-shirt.; 2 The socks cost less than the dress./The dress costs more than the socks.; 3 The coat costs more than the shoes./The shoes cost less than the coat.; 4 The pants cost less than the tie./The tie costs more than the pants.

Activity C

1 checks; 2 skirt; 3 shirt; 4 receipt; 5 cash; 6 small; 7 pink; 8 trousers

Unit 8 Lesson 1

Activity A 1 fly; 2 take; 3 walk

Activity B
1 They're in Central Park in New York.; 2 They want to go to the Tourist Information Center in Times Square.; 3 They can take the bus or the subway.; 4 No, she doesn't. Muhammad prefers to walk.

Lesson 2

Activity A
library; subway station; school; church; train station; bus stop; post office; supermarket

Activity B
1 b; 2 b; 3 b; 4 a

Lesson 3

Activity A
1 I want to take the bus. Where is the bus stop?; 2 I want to take the train. Where is the train station?; 3 I want to take the subway. Where is the subway station?

Activity B
1 Where is the train station?; 2 How do I get to the subway station?; 3 The station is near the school.; 4 Let's buy a map.

Activity C
Answers may vary. Possible answers:
Well, first go to the bus stop across the street and take bus number 9. Get off the bus at Penn Station. Then take the train to Boston.

Your Turn
Answers will vary.

Lesson 4

Activity A
Here I am in Canada. It was a long journey but the weather is very nice. Yesterday I took the plane at eight thirty and I arrived here at 10 o'clock in the morning. I went to the hotel and went to bed! I slept for one hour and then went downtown. I saw a lot of interesting buildings and stores there. I bought some postcards and ate a hamburger and then I came back to the hotel.

Activity B
1 I ate breakfast at 8:00 AM.; 2 Monica took the bus. ; 3 Jung Yun was in Korea.; 4 We had a nice hotel.

Lesson 5

Activity A 1 a; 2 b; 3 a; 4 a

Activity B 12 PM; 1 PM

Lesson 6

Activity A 1 b; 2 d; 3 e; 4 a; 5 c

Activity B
1 suitcase; 2 plane; 3 airport; 4 passport; 5 ticket

Lesson 7

Activity A
1 My flight arrived at 12:30 PM.; 2 Where's the departure gate?; 3 How much does the ticket cost?; 4 I want to go to a nice hotel.

Activity B 1 a; 2 b; 3 a

Activity C
1 The flight to Seattle was at 5:25 PM.; 2 Flight EZY5259 to Los Angeles departed at 4:35 PM.; 3 Flight VZX7250 arrived in Miami.; 4 The flight to Memphis was at 5:20 PM.

Your Turn
Answers may vary. Possible answer:
The next flight for New York is number 1699. It departs at 10:23 AM and arrives at 1:30 PM.

Lesson 8

Activity A
1 My flight will arrive at Gate 10.; 2 When is my flight going to depart?; 3 When are you going to go on your vacation?; 4 I'll meet you at the train station.

Activity B
Answers will vary.

Activity C 1 b; 2 b; 3 b; 4 a

Review

Activity A
1 went; 2 walked; 3 looked; 4 bought; 5 got; 6 were

Activity B
Tomorrow I'm going to London, England. My flight leaves at 8 o'clock in the morning. I must be at the airport at six o'clock. It's very early! I have my ticket and my passport and my luggage. I arrive in London at 10 o'clock and then I must find the bus to go to the hotel. The hotel is near Trafalgar Square. It's behind a church. Tomorrow I want to visit/to go to the National Gallery and then go to/visit the Tate Museum. I need some English money. Where did I put it?

Activity C
1 a; 2 a; 3 a; 4 b

Challenge

bring	brought
see	saw
wear	wore
read	read
pay	paid
put	put
fly	flew
speak	spoke
write	wrote
swim	swam
cost	cost

Unit 9 Lesson 1

Activity A 1 b; 2 a; 3 b; 4 a

Activity B
1 worked; 2 wrote; 3 culture; 4 will start

Activity C 1 will; 2 won't; 3 will; 4 won't

Lesson 2

Activity A
school: classroom; student; teacher
work: job; office; employer

Activity B Answers will vary.

Activity C
a: a classroom; b: a student; c: a teacher
a: an office; b: a journalist; c: a journalist

Lesson 3

Activity A
1 I'm a teacher.; 2 I'm a journalist.; 3 I want to be a journalist.; 4 I want to be a teacher.

Activity B
1 What do you do (for a living)?; 2 I'm a journalist.; 3 What do you want to do later on in life?; 4 I want to be a teacher.; 5 I am a salesperson.

Your Turn
Answers may vary. Possible answers:
What do you teach? I teach math.; Where do you teach? I teach in a high school.; How old are your students? They're teenagers.; What do you like about your job? I like my students.; What don't you like about your job? I don't like grading tests.

Lesson 4

Activity A
1 has worked; 2 Have they worked; 3 have worked; 4 have you worked; 5 I've worked

Activity B
1 has she lived here; 2 have they lived; 3 have you studied English; 4 you worked as a police officer for a long time

Your Turn Answers will vary.

Lesson 5

Activity A
1 human resources coordinator; 2 three years; 3 NatWest Bank; 4 Job Consulting Inc.; 5 gain more experience in a larger company and to have more responsibility.

Activity B
The first sentence describes a past action. He worked at NatWest before but he doesn't work there now. The second sentence describes an action that started in the past but is still happening. He worked there before and he works there now.

Lesson 6

Activity A 1 a; 2 b; 3 a; 4 b

Activity B
1 business; 2 salary; 3 assistant; 4 company; 5 boss; 6 secretary; 7 job

Your Turn Answers will vary.

Lesson 7

Activity A
1 Why do you want to be a journalist?; 2 I like to help other people.; 3 How long have you worked in a big company?; 4 I've worked at my company for two years.

Activity B
1 hotter; 2 better; 3 more expensive; 4 faster; 5 more boring

Activity C
Answers will vary.

Lesson 8

Activity A

Base Form	Simple Past	Past Participle
buy	bought	bought
do	did	done
drive	drove	driven
eat	ate	eaten
go	went	gone
get	got	got
leave	left	left
say	said	said
speak	spoke	spoken
take	took	taken
write	wrote	written

Activity B
1 have read; 2 has taught; 3 have been; 4 have had; 5 has eaten; 6 has done

Review

Activity A 1 b; 2 a; 3 a; 4 a

Activity B
1 When will they work?; 2 Where did she work?; 3 Why does he work?; 4 What does he do (for a living)?; 5 Which office does she have?

Activity C
1 The United States is bigger than New Zealand.; 2 The Nile River is longer than the Mississippi River.; 3 Madrid is colder than Hanoi in winter.; 4 The Eiffel Tower is taller than Big Ben.

Activity D Answers will vary.

Challenge
All three forms (base, past tense and past participle) are the same.

Unit 10 Lesson 1

Activity A

1 b; 2 a; 3 b; 4 b

Activity B

1 Yes, he will.; 2 Pick up her clothes.; 3 Tidy up the living room.; 4 Clean and paint.

Lesson 2

Activity A

Answers will vary.

Activity B

1 living room; 2 kitchen; 3 bedroom; 4 bathroom; 5 dining room

Lesson 3

Activity A

1 Can you give me a hand?/Can you help me?; 2 I'm sorry, I can't help you (I'm afraid); .3 What do you want me to do?; 4 I'll do it right away.

Activity B

2; 3; 4; 1

Lesson 4

Activity A

1 a; 2 b; 3 b; 4 a

Activity B

Organize your closet!; Paint the wall!; Pick up your clothes!; Clean the floor!

Lesson 5

Activity A

1 a; 2 b; 3 b; 4 b

Activity B

1 They went to a rock concert.; 2 Yes, they had a good time at the concert.; 3 She went shopping yesterday.; 4 After shopping she went to a nightclub.

Activity C

1 The day before yesterday she went to a rock concert.; 2 Yesterday she went shopping.; 3 Last night she went to a nightclub.

Lesson 6

Activity A

1 a nightclub; 2 a movie theater; 3 a theater; 4 a concert

Activity B

1 yesterday; 2 the day before yesterday; 3 last week; 4 last night

Activity C

Answers will vary.

Lesson 7

Activity A

1 What did you do last week?; 2 What do you want to do?; 3 I want to go out.; 4 I want to stay at home.

Activity B

3; 2; 1; 6; 7; 5

Ed decides to stay home tonight.

Activity C

Answers will vary.

Your Turn

Answers will vary.

Lesson 8

Activity A

1 were painting; 2 was making; 3 Were you watching; 4 was eating

Activity B

1 Scott was working.; 2 Katrina and Carl were talking.; 3 Mia was shopping.; 4 Monique was looking at a map.

Your Turn

Answers will vary.

Review

Activity A

1 film; 2 dance; 3 paint; 4 kitchen; 5 bathroom

Activity B

1 d; 2 f; 3 c; 4 e; 5 a; 6 b

Activity C

1 a; 2 b; 3 a; 4 b

Activity D

1 went; 2 I'll/I will; 3 Have you lived; 4 make; 5 cleaned

Challenge

Answers will vary.

Unit 11 Lesson 1

Activity A 1 a; 2 b; 3 b; 4 b

Activity B 1 a; 2 b; 3 a

Activity C

Answers may vary. Possible answer:
Hi Melanie! I'm not sick anymore. Let's play tennis tomorrow/on Sunday. Roberto

Lesson 2

Activity A

1 swimming; 2 tennis; 3 soccer; 4 cycling

Activity B

alone: cycling; swimming
with other people: baseball; soccer; tennis

Your Turn

Answers will vary.

Lesson 3

Activity A

1 I'm in good health.; 2 I'm in good shape. ;3 How do you feel?; 4 I want to lose weight.

Activity B 1 a; 2 b; 3 b; 4 a

Your Turn

Answers will vary.

Lesson 4

Activity A

1 b; 2 a; 3 b; 4 a

Activity B

1 Marta loves riding her bicycle, and she loves playing tennis.; 2 We felt tired, so we didn't go to the gym.; 3 I like soccer, but I don't play it very well.; 4 Simon was bored, so he decided to watch baseball on TV.

Your Turn

Answers may vary. Possible answers:
1 It's going to rain, so you should bring an umbrella.; 2 They'll cook dinner, and then they'll eat.; 3 He's cleaning the floor, but he's not going to do the dishes.; 4 She's studying, and she's learning a lot.

Lesson 5

Activity A 1 a; 2 a; 3 b; 4 b

Activity B 1 a; 2 a; 3 a; 4 a

Activity C

temperature; headache; coughs and sneezes; (doctor's) prescription

Lesson 6

Activity A 1 b; 2 b; 3 a; 4 b

Activity B

1 Antonio has a stomachache.; 2 Teresa has a cold.; 3 Arnaud has a headache.; 4 Nina has a toothache.

Your Turn

Answers may vary. Possible answers:
1 Antonio needs to stop eating.; 2 Teresa needs to see a doctor.; 3 Arnaud needs to take aspirin.; 4 Nina needs to see a dentist.

Lesson 7

Activity A

1 My wrist hurts.; 2 Her back hurts.; 3 Her feet hurt.; 4 His arm hurts.

Activity B

1 myself; 2 herself; 3 ourselves; 4 himself; 5 themselves

Your Turn Answers will vary.

Lesson 8

Activity A

1 F; 2 T; 3 F; 4 F

Activity B

Answers will vary.

Activity C

1 rarely; 2 usually; 3 never; 4 often

Your Turn Answers will vary.

Review

Activity A

Jim	I want to lose weight.
Mick	I want to gain weight.
Jim	I'm in bad shape.
Mick	I'm in good shape.
Jim	I feel better.
Mick	I feel worse.
Jim	I never take medicine.
Mick	I always take medicine.

Activity B

1 I have a headache.; 2 I played tennis yesterday.; 3 She plays baseball well.; 4 We exercise a lot.; 5 I hurt myself./He hurt himself.; 6 They never go swimming.

Activity C

1 cycling; 2 tennis; 3 headache; 4 medicine; 5 temperature; 6 dentist

Challenge Answers will vary.

Interior

p. 6: © Orange Line Media 2008/Shutterstock, Inc., © Jason Stitt 2008/ Shutterstock, Inc., © Jason Stitt 2008/Shutterstock, Inc., p. 7: © Dmitriy Shironosov 2008/Shutterstock, Inc., © 2008/Comstock, © 2008/Comstock, , p. 8: © Awe Inspiring Images/Shutterstock, Inc., © Lars Christensen/Shutterstock, Inc., p. 9: © Lisa F. Young/Shutterstock, Inc., © Bobby Deal/RealDealPhoto/ Shutterstock, Inc., © 2008/Ablestock, © 2008/Comstock, © 2008/Comstock, © Yuri Arcurs 2008/Shutterstock, Inc., © Konstantynov 2008/Shutterstock, Inc., © Getty Images 2008/Jupiter Images, © 3drenderings 2010/Shutterstock, © S.M. 2010/Shutterstock, Inc., p. 11: © Sandra G/Shutterstock, Inc., © Nayashkova Olga 2010/Shutterstock, Inc., © Lukas Wroblewski 2008/ Shutterstock, Inc., © Pilar Echevarria 2008/Shutterstock, Inc., © Edyta Pawlowska 2008/Shutterstock, Inc., © matin 2010/Shutterstock, Inc., p. 12: © S-Borisov 2010/Shutterstock, Inc., p. 13: © Yuri Arcurs/Shutterstock, Inc., © DmitriyShironosov 2008/Shutterstock, Inc., p. 15: © Pavel Sazonov 2008/ Shutterstock, Inc., © Tyler Olson 2010/Shutterstock, Inc., © Steve Allen 2010/ Jupiter Images, Inc., © Christopher Parypa 2010/Shutterstock, Inc., © Christopher Parypa 2010/Shutterstock, Inc., © Elena Elisseeva 2008/Shutterstock,Inc., © Kiselev Andrey Valerevich/Shutterstock,Inc., p. 16: © photobank.ch 2008/ Shutterstock, Inc., © photobank.ch 2008/Shutterstock, Inc., © Yuri Arcurs 2008/ Shutterstock, Inc., © vgstudio 2008/Shutterstock, Inc., © BESTWEB 2008/ Shutterstock, Inc., © Kirill Vorobyev 2008/Shutterstock, Inc., © Alexey Nikolaew 2008/Shutterstock, Inc., © fckncg 2008/Shutterstock, Inc., © Hannu Lilvaar 2008/Shutterstock, Inc., © SOMATUSCAN 2010/Shutterstock, Inc., © Denise Kappa 2008/Shutterstock, Inc., © Paul Matthew 2008/Shutterstock, Inc., © Monkey Business Images 2010/Shutterstock, Inc., photoshop document, © Arthur Eugene Preston 2008/Shutterstock, Inc., © Rob Wilson 2008/Shutterstock, Inc., © Kristian Sekulic 2008/Shutterstock, Inc., © Sandy Maya Matzen 2008/ Shutterstock, Inc., © Galina Barskaya 2008/Shutterstock,Inc., © Luminis 2008/ Shutterstock, Inc. , p. 17: © Nagy-Bagoly Arpad/Shutterstock, Inc., © Yuri Arcurs 2008/Shutterstock, Inc., © Dmitriy Shironosov 2008/Shutterstock, Inc., photoshop document, © Erik Lam 2008/Shutterstock, Inc., © Suponev VladimirMihajlovich 2008/Shutterstock, Inc., © mlorenz 2008/Shutterstock, Inc., © Christopher Parypa 2010/Shutterstock, Inc., , © Andresr 2008/Shutterstock, Inc., © Andresr 2008/Shutterstock, Inc., © vgstudio 2008/Shutterstock, Inc., © Yuri Arcurs 2008/Shutterstock, Inc., © Martina Ebel 2010/Shutterstock, Inc., © Martina Ebel 2010/Shutterstock, Inc., © melkerw 2008/Shutterstock, Inc., p. 18: © SamDCruz 2008/Shutterstock, Inc., , p. 20: © Scott Waldron/Shutterstock, Inc., p. 21: © 2008 Jupiter Images, Inc., © Andy Lim 2008/Shutterstock, Inc., © 2008 Jupiter Images, Inc., © 2008 Jupiter Images, Inc., © 2008 Jupiter Images, Inc., © 2008 Jupiter Images, Inc., p. 22: © 2008 Jupiter Images, Inc., p. 23: © Nick Stubbs 2008/Shutterstock, Inc., © AND, Inc./Shutterstock, Inc., © Tomasz Pietryszek 2008/Shutterstock, Inc., © Michael Ransburg 2008/Shutterstock, Inc., © Philip Date 2008/Shutterstock, Inc., © Raia 2008/Shutterstock, Inc., p. 24: © Nenad C – tataleka 2010/Shutterstock, Inc., © Steve Luker 2008/Shutterstock, Inc., © MaxFX 2008/Shutterstock, Inc., © Steve Luker 2008/Shutterstock, Inc., © MaxFX 2008/Shutterstock, Inc., ©Bart Everett/Shutterstock, Inc., p. 25: © Laurent Hamels 2008/Shutterstock, Inc., p. 26: © Konstantin Remizov/Shutterstock, Inc., p. 27: © Franco Deriu 2008/Shutterstock, Inc., p. 28: © GinaSanders 2008/Shutterstock, Inc., © Getty Images 2008/Jupiter Images, Inc., © Rafa Irusta 2008/Shutterstock, Inc., © Morgan Lane Photography 2008/Shutterstock, Inc., © Tomasz Trojanowski 2008/Shutterstock, Inc., © Rafa Irusta 2008/Shutterstock, Inc., created by designer, © George Dolgikh 2008/Shutterstock, Inc., © tinatka 2008/ Shutterstock, Inc., © David Hyde 2008/Shutterstock, Inc., © Julian Rovagnati 2008/Shutterstock, Inc., © Elena Ray 2008/Shutterstock, Inc., © tinatka 2008/ Shutterstock, Inc., © J. Helgason/Shutterstock, Inc., p. 30: © Thinkstock 2008/ Comstock, © Phil Date 2008/Shutterstock, Inc., p. 31: © Imageshop.com, © Simone van den Berg 2008/Shutterstock, Inc., © Creatas 2008/Jupiter Images, Inc., p. 32: created by designer, © Mike Flippo 2008/Shutterstock, Inc., p. 33: © Simon Krzic 2008/Shutterstock, Inc., © Edyta Pawlowska 2008/Shutterstock, Inc., © MWProductions 2008/Shutterstock, Inc., © Dusaleev Viatcheslav 2008/ Shutterstock, Inc., p. 34: © Andresr 2008/Shutterstock, Inc., © T-Design 2008/ Shutterstock,Inc., © Jason Stitt 2008/Shutterstock, Inc., © Aetherial Images 2008/ Shutterstock, Inc., , p. 35: © Vibrant Image Studio/Shutterstock, Inc., © iofoto 2008/Shutterstock, Inc., © iofoto 2008/Shutterstock, Inc., © iofoto 2008/ Shutterstock, Inc., © Ersler Dmitry 2008/Shutterstock, Inc., © Jeanne Hatch 2008/Shutterstock, Inc., © Jaren Jai Wicklund2008/Shutterstock, Inc., © Adam Borkowski 2008/Shutterstock, Inc., p. 36: © Lisa F. Young/Shutterstock, Inc., ©

Comstock Images 2008, © Yuri Arcurs/Shutterstock, Inc., , © Comstock Images 2008, © Martin Valigursky 2008/Shutterstock, Inc., © Vibrant Image Studio 2008/Shutterstock, Inc., © Monkey Business Images2008/Shutterstock, Inc., © Denise Kappa 2008/Shutterstock, Inc., © Monkey Business Images2008/ Shutterstock, Inc., © Monkey Business Images2008/Shutterstock, Inc., p. 37: © Doctor Kan 2008/Shutterstock, Inc., © Carme Balcells 2008/Shutterstock, Inc., © Sandra Gligorijevic 2008/Shutterstock, Inc., © Kurhan 2008/Shutterstock, Inc., © Simon Krzic 2008/Shutterstock, Inc., © Carme Balcells 2008/Shutterstock, Inc., © Kirill Vorobyev 2008/Shutterstock, Inc., © Allgord 2008/Shutterstock, Inc., © Konstantin Sutyagin 2008/Shutterstock, Inc., © Sandra Gligorijevic 2008/ Shutterstock, Inc., © Andriy Goncharenko 2008/Shutterstock, Inc., © Dagmara Ponikiewska 2008/Shutterstock, Inc., © KSR 2008/Shutterstock, Inc., p. 38: © Lisa F. Young/Shutterstock, Inc., © Najin 2008/Shutterstock, Inc., © Elena Ray 2008/Shutterstock, Inc., © Elena Ray 2008/Shutterstock, Inc., p. 39: © Losevsky Pavel/Shutterstock, Inc., © Elena Ray 2008/Shutterstock, Inc., © Vitezslav Halamka 2008/Shutterstock, Inc., © Robyn Mackenzie 2008/Shutterstock, Inc., p. 40: © Jaimie Duplass 2008/Shutterstock, Inc., © Serghei Starus 2008/ Shutterstock, Inc., © Philip Date 2008/Shutterstock, Inc., p. 41: © Monkey Business Images 2008/Shutterstock, Inc., © Sandra Gligorijevic 2008/ Shutterstock, Inc., © Monkey Business Images 2008/Shutterstock, Inc., © Konstantin Sutyagin 2008/Shutterstock, Inc., p. 42: © Peter Polak 2008/ Shutterstock, Inc., © RexRover2008/Shutterstock, Inc., © Valentyn Volkov 2008/ Shutterstock, Inc., © imageZebra 2008/Shutterstock, Inc., © Rudchenko Liliia 2008/Shutterstock, Inc., p. 43: © Edyta Pawlowska/Shutterstock, Inc., © Dusan Zidar 2008/Shutterstock, Inc., © Supri Suharjoto 2008/Shutterstock, Inc., © Monkey Business Images 2008/Shutterstock, Inc., © Edw 2008/Shutterstock, Inc., p. 44: © Ana Blazic/Shutterstock, Inc., © Alexander Shalamov 2008/ Shutterstock, Inc. © BlueOrange Studio 2008/Shutterstock, Inc., © Phil Date 2008/Shutterstock, Inc., © Dragan Trifunovic2008/Shutterstock, Inc., p. 45: © Steve Luker/Shutterstock, Inc., © Andre Nantel 2008/Shutterstock, Inc., p. 46: © Jackie Carvey 2008/Shutterstock, Inc., © Creatas 2008/Comstock, Inc., © sarsmis 2010/Shutterstock,Inc., © Viktor1 2008/Shutterstock, Inc., © Marco Mayer 2010/Shutterstock,Inc., © Liv Friis-Larsen2008/Shutterstock, Inc., © Bochkarev Photography 2008/Shutterstock, Inc., © Sarune Zurbaite 2008/ Shutterstock, Inc., © Kheng Guan Toh/Shutterstock, Inc., p. 47: © Rene Jansa 2008/Shutterstock, Inc., © 2008/Comstock, © Rudchenko Liliia 2008/Shutterstock, Inc., © Valentin Mosichev 2008/Shutterstock, Inc., © Olga Lyubkina 2008/ Shutterstock, Inc., © Joe Gough 2008/Shutterstock, Inc., © Paul Maguire 2008/ Shutterstock, Inc., © Viktor1 2008/Shutterstock, Inc., p. 48: © 2008/Comstock, © Keith Wheatley/Shutterstock, Inc., p. 51: © John R. Smith 2008/Shutterstock, Inc., © John R. Smith 2008/Shutterstock, Inc., p. 52: © Marcel Mooij/ Shutterstock, Inc., © Victor Burnside/Shutterstock, Inc., © Ekaterina Starshaya 2008/Shutterstock, Inc., © Zaporozchenko Yury 2008/Shutterstock,Inc., © Ronald van der Beek 2008/Shutterstock, Inc., © Yakobchuk Vasyl 2008/ Shutterstock, Inc., p. 53: © Kruchankova Maya/Shutterstock, Inc., © iofoto 2008/ Shutterstock, Inc., © pdtnc 2008/Shutterstock, Inc., © Yuri Arcurs 2008/ Shutterstock, Inc., © Stas Volik 2008/Shutterstock, Inc., © Getty Images 2008/ Jupiter Images, Inc., © Jeff Gynane 2008/Shutterstock, Inc., , p. 54: © Robert Kneschke 2010/Shutterstock, Inc., © Robert Kneschke 2010/Shutterstock, Inc., © Robert Kneschke 2010/Shutterstock, Inc., © Robert Kneschke 2010/Shutterstock, Inc., © dukibu 2010/Shutterstock, Inc., © Kiselev Andrey Valerevich/Shutterstock, Inc., , p. 55: © Val Thoermer 2008/Shutterstock, Inc., © Andresr 2008/ Shutterstock, Inc., © Lorraine Swanson2008/Shutterstock, Inc., p. 56: © Ilike/ Shutterstock, Inc., © Comstock 2008/Jupiter Images, Inc., © Kiselev Andrey Valrevich 2008/Shutterstock, Inc., © Anton Gvozdikov 2008/Shutterstock, Inc., © Liv Friis-Larsen 2008/Shutterstock, Inc., p. 57: © Anatoliy Samara/Shutterstock, Inc., © Patricia Hofmeester 2008/Shutterstock, Inc., © yuyuangc 2008/ Shutterstock, Inc., © Robyn Mackenzie 2008/Shutterstock, Inc., © stocksnapp 2008/Shutterstock, Inc., © Andrew N. Ilyasov 2008/Shutterstock, Inc., © Austra 2008/Shutterstock, Inc., © miskolin 2008/Shutterstock, Inc., © Michael Nguyen 2008/Shutterstock, Inc., p. 59: © children photos 2010/Shutterstock, Inc., © Sergiy Guk 2010/Shutterstock, Inc., © Mircea BEZERGHEANU 2010/ Shutterstock, Inc., , © Viktor Pryymachuk 2008/Shutterstock,Inc., p. 60: © Carlos E. Santa Maria/Shutterstock,Inc., © Gladskikh Tatiana 2008/Shutterstock, Inc., © istihza 2008/Shutterstock, Inc., © Andrey Armyagov 2008/Shutterstock, Inc., © Karkas 2008/Shutterstock, Inc., © Terekhov Igor 2008/Shutterstock, Inc., © Terekhov Igor 2008/Shutterstock, Inc., © Terekhov Igor 2008/Shutterstock, Inc., © Karkas 2008/Shutterstock, Inc., © Karkas 2008/Shutterstock, Inc., © istihza 2008/Shutterstock, Inc., p. 61: © Andrey Armyagov/Shutterstock, Inc., © Janos